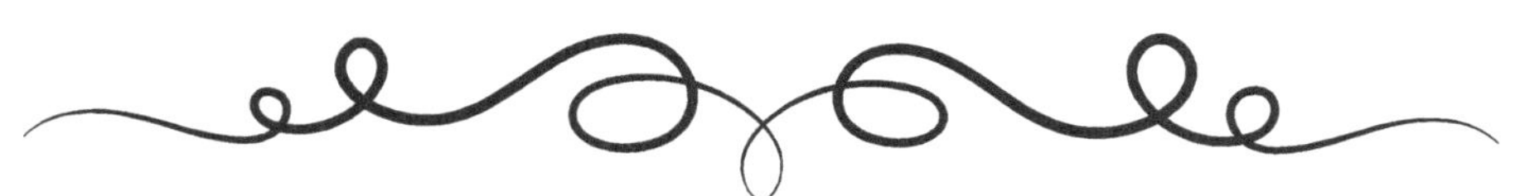

If you are alive, you are capable of anything and nothing is impossible!
Inner beauty is a concept that refers to a person's personality, values, beliefs, and character traits. These traits make us good, kind, and compassionate human beings. It is often contrasted with physical beauty, which refers to a person's external appearance.
Always be kind to others and it will come back to you!

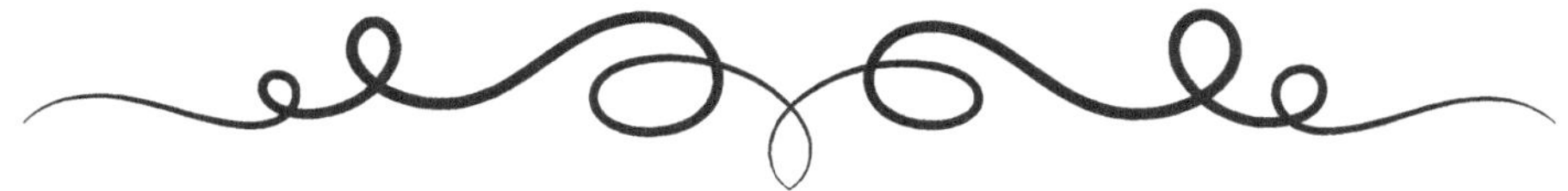

# I AM A BEAUTIFUL PERSON INSIDE AND OUT

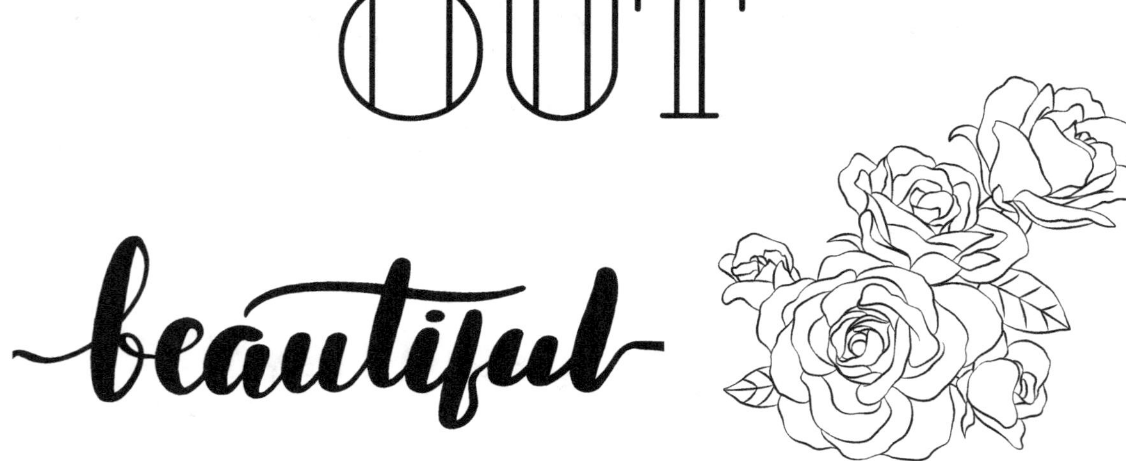

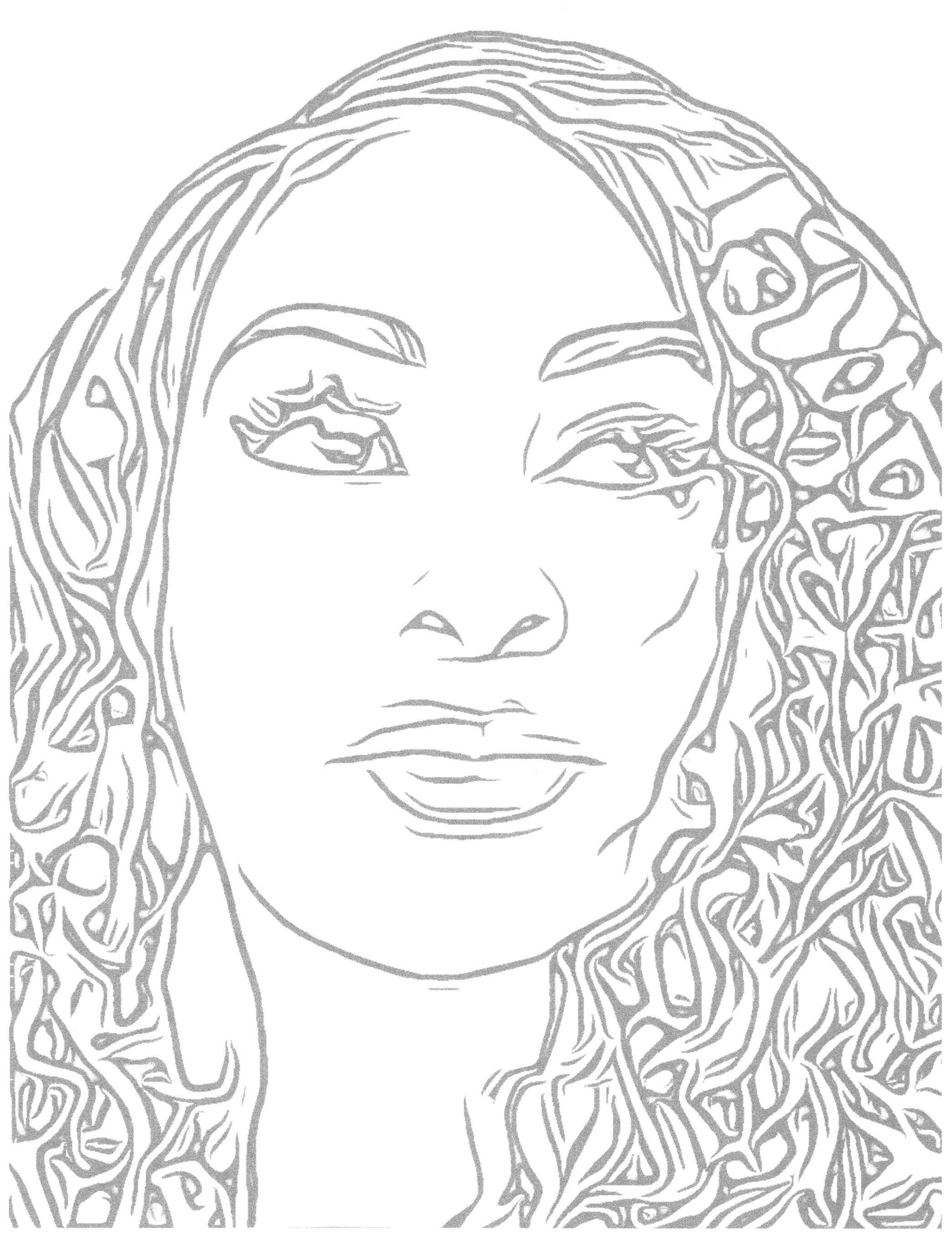

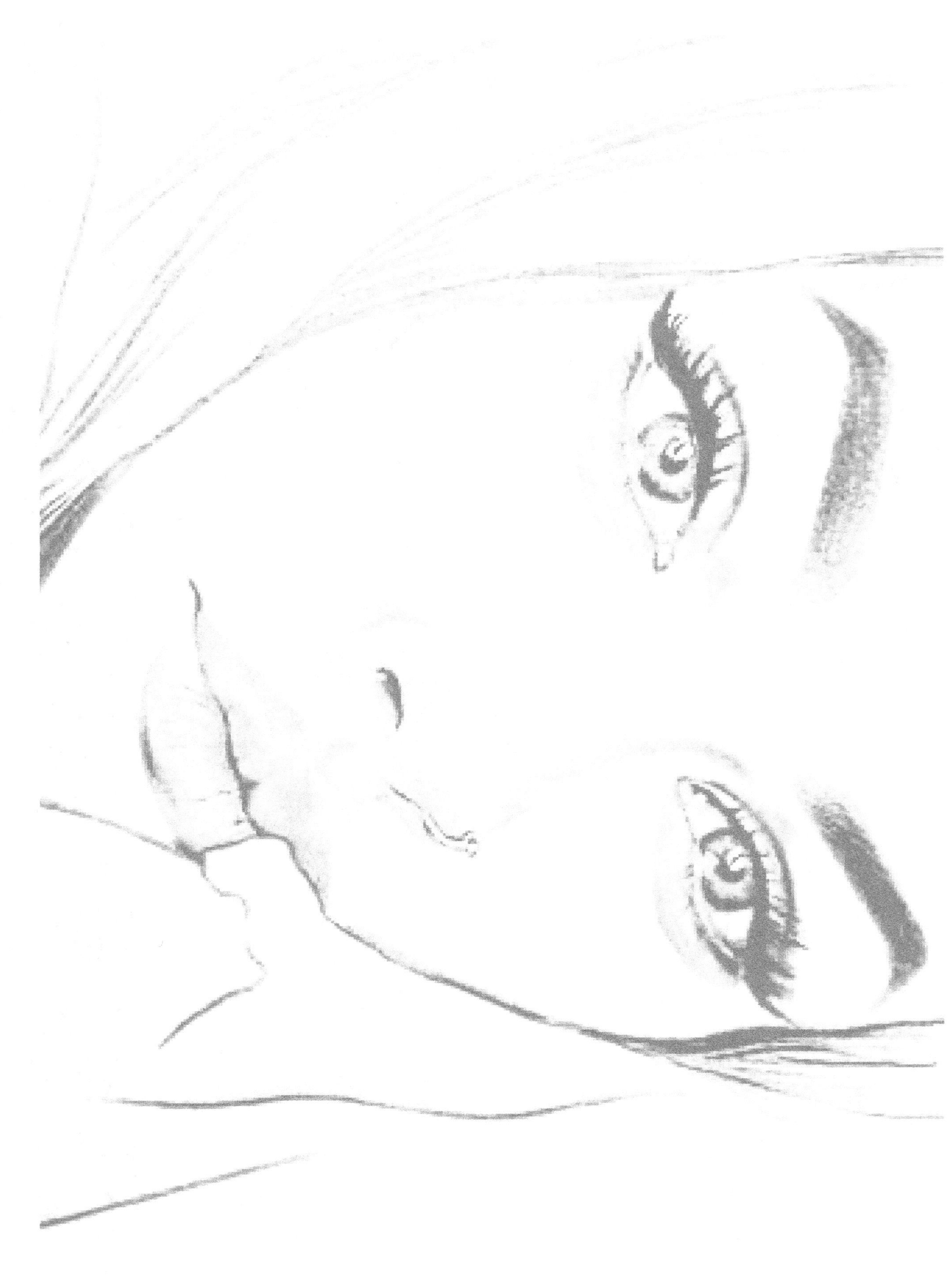

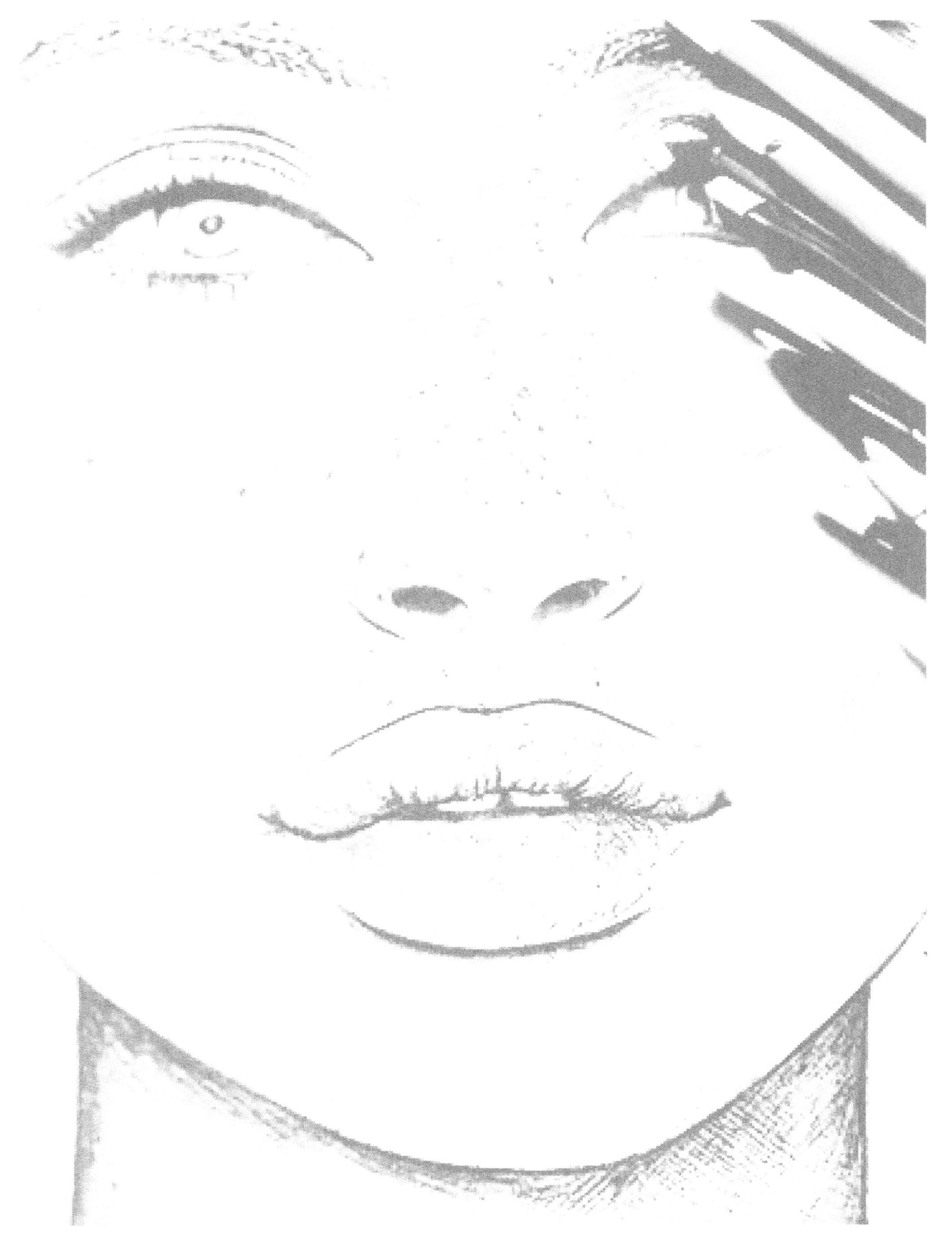

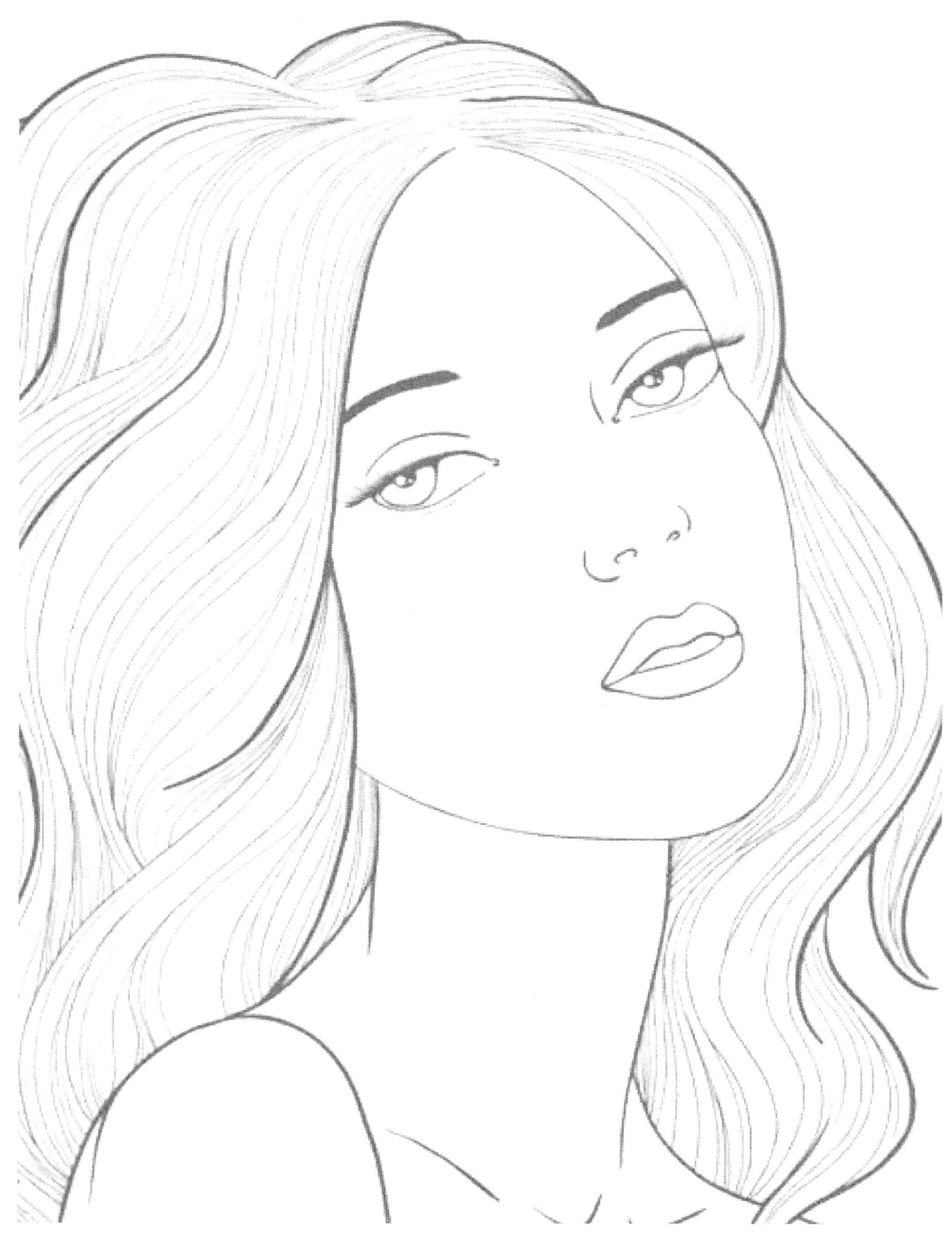

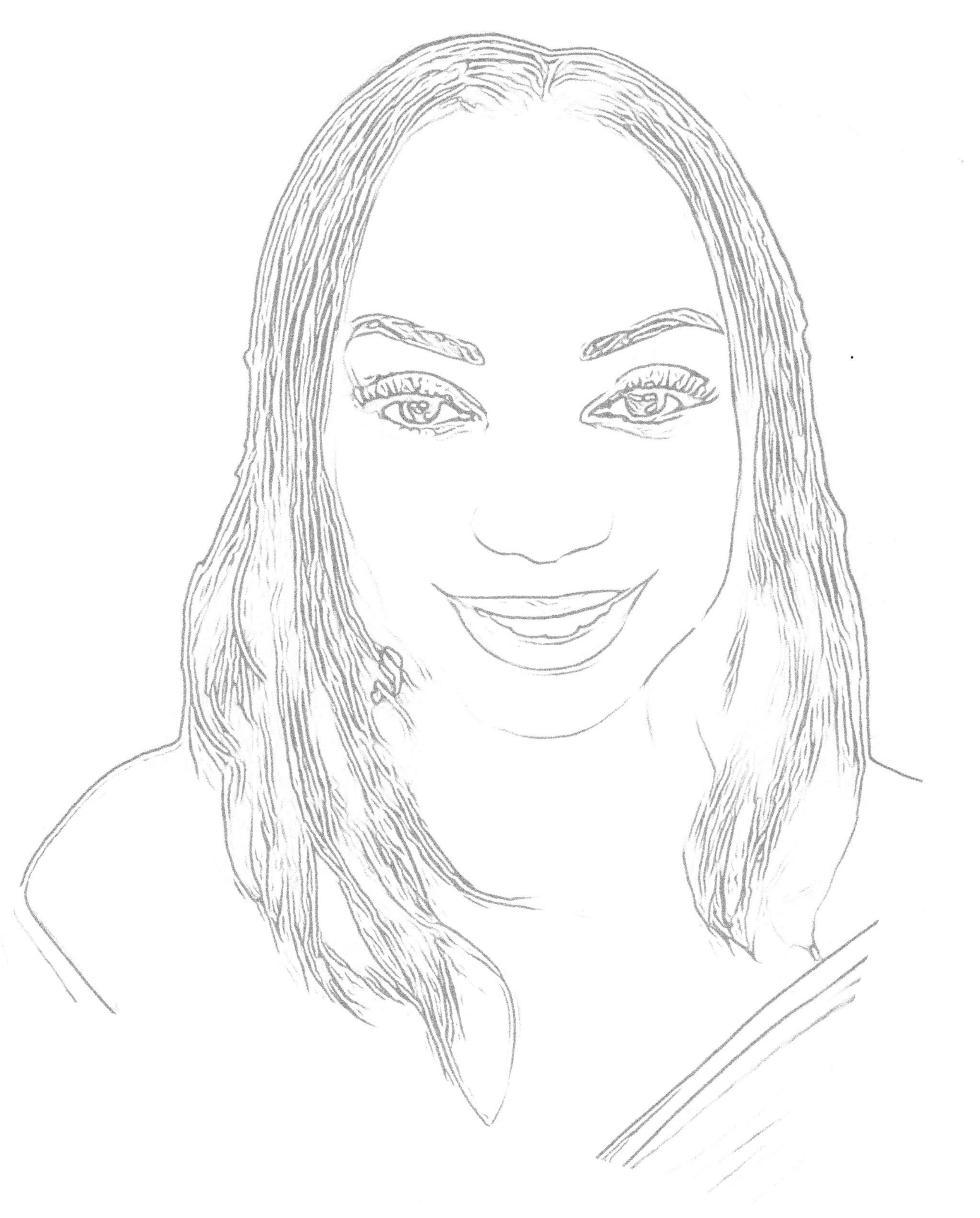

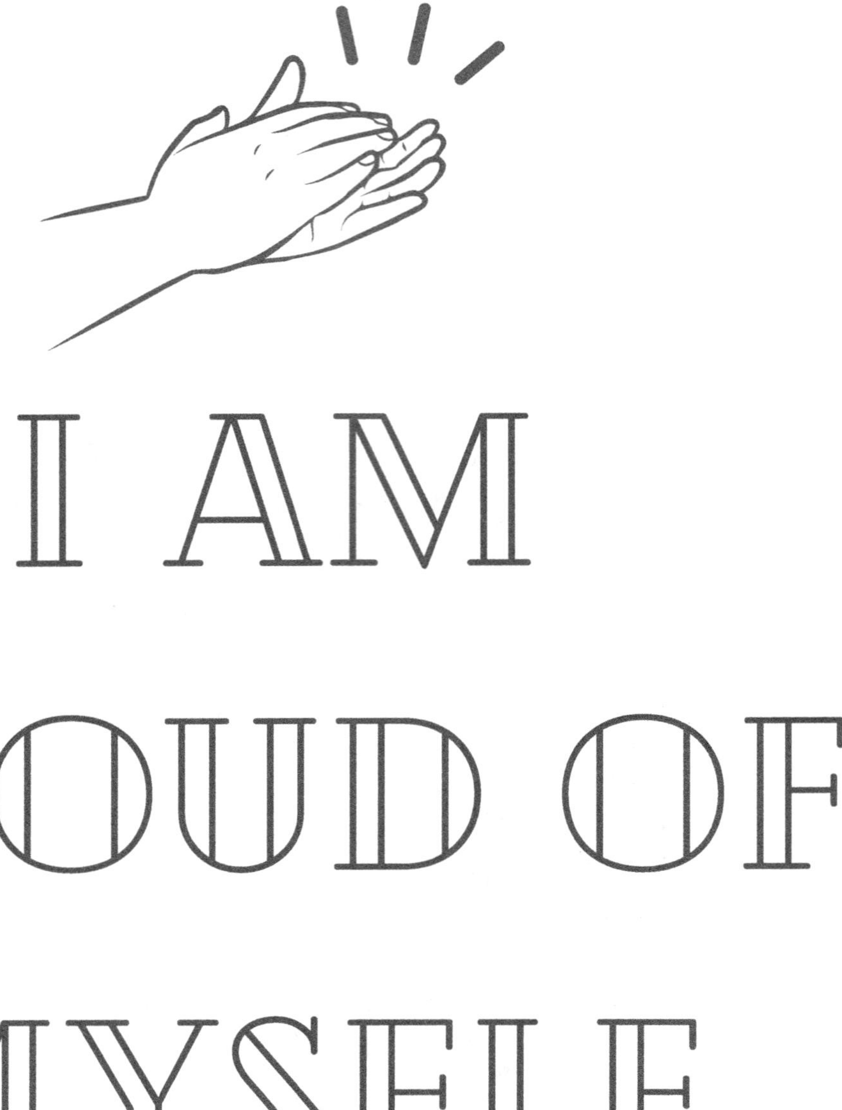

# I AM
# PROUD OF
# MYSELF

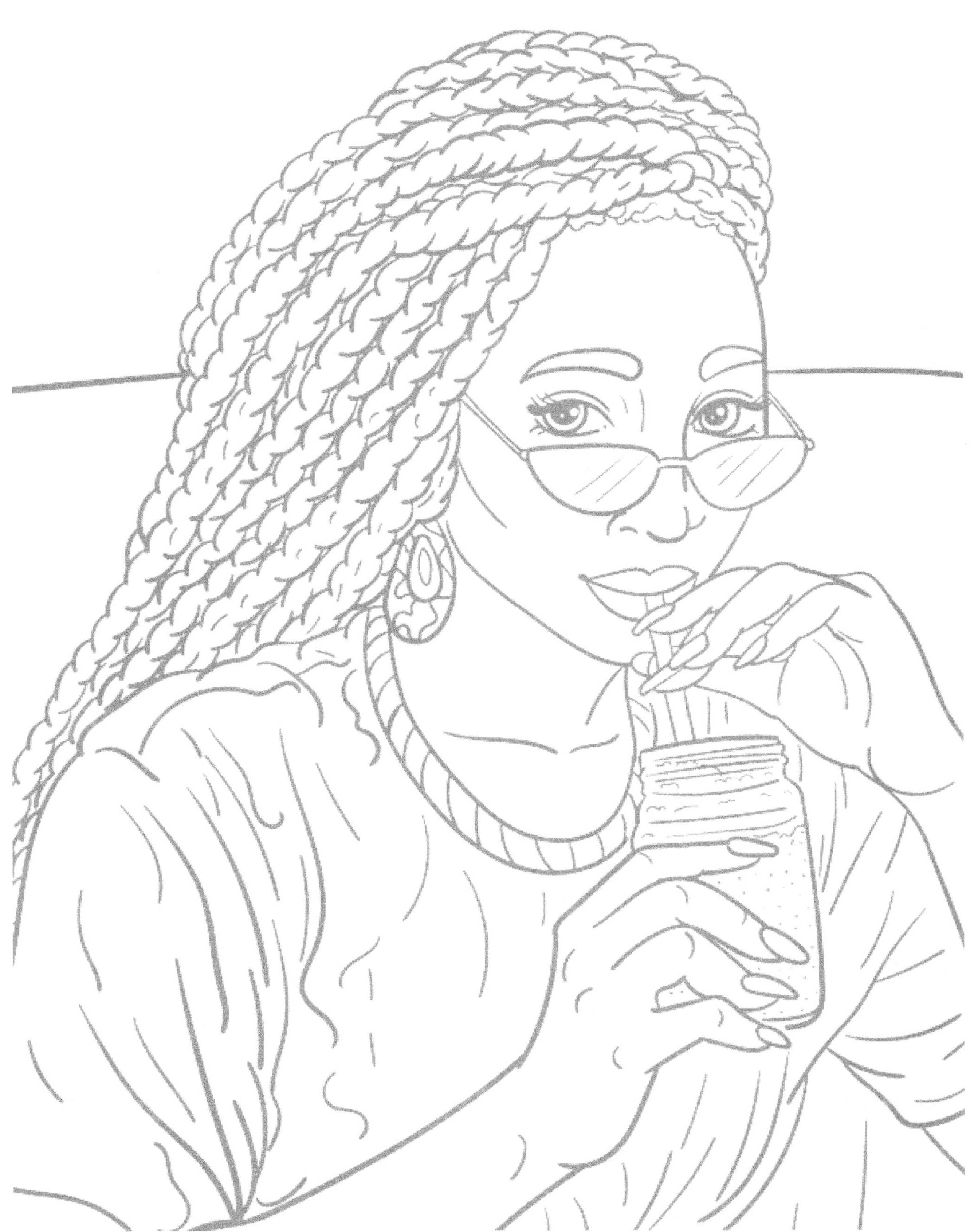

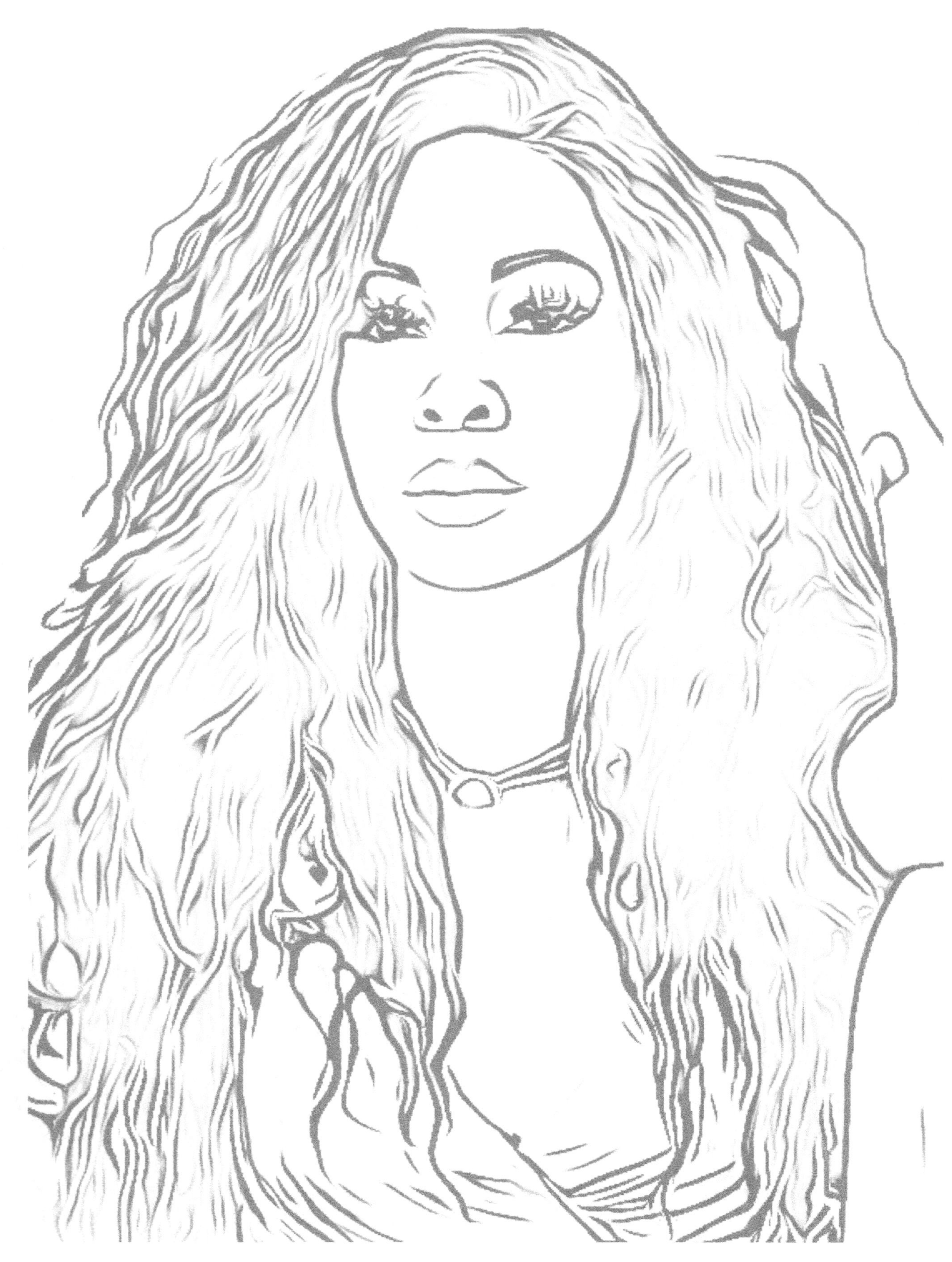

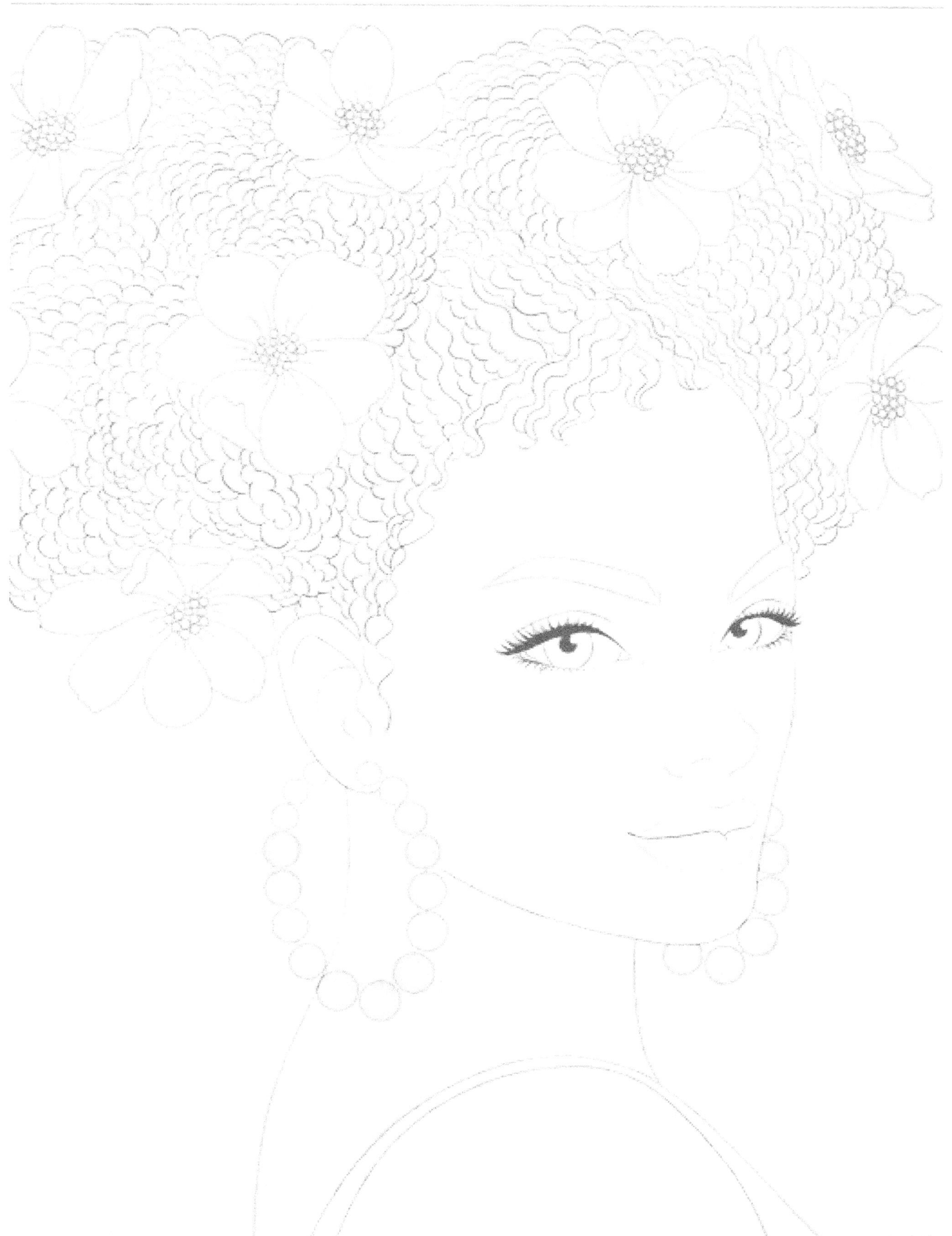

# I HAVE ENOUGH. I DO ENOUGH. I AM ENOUGH.

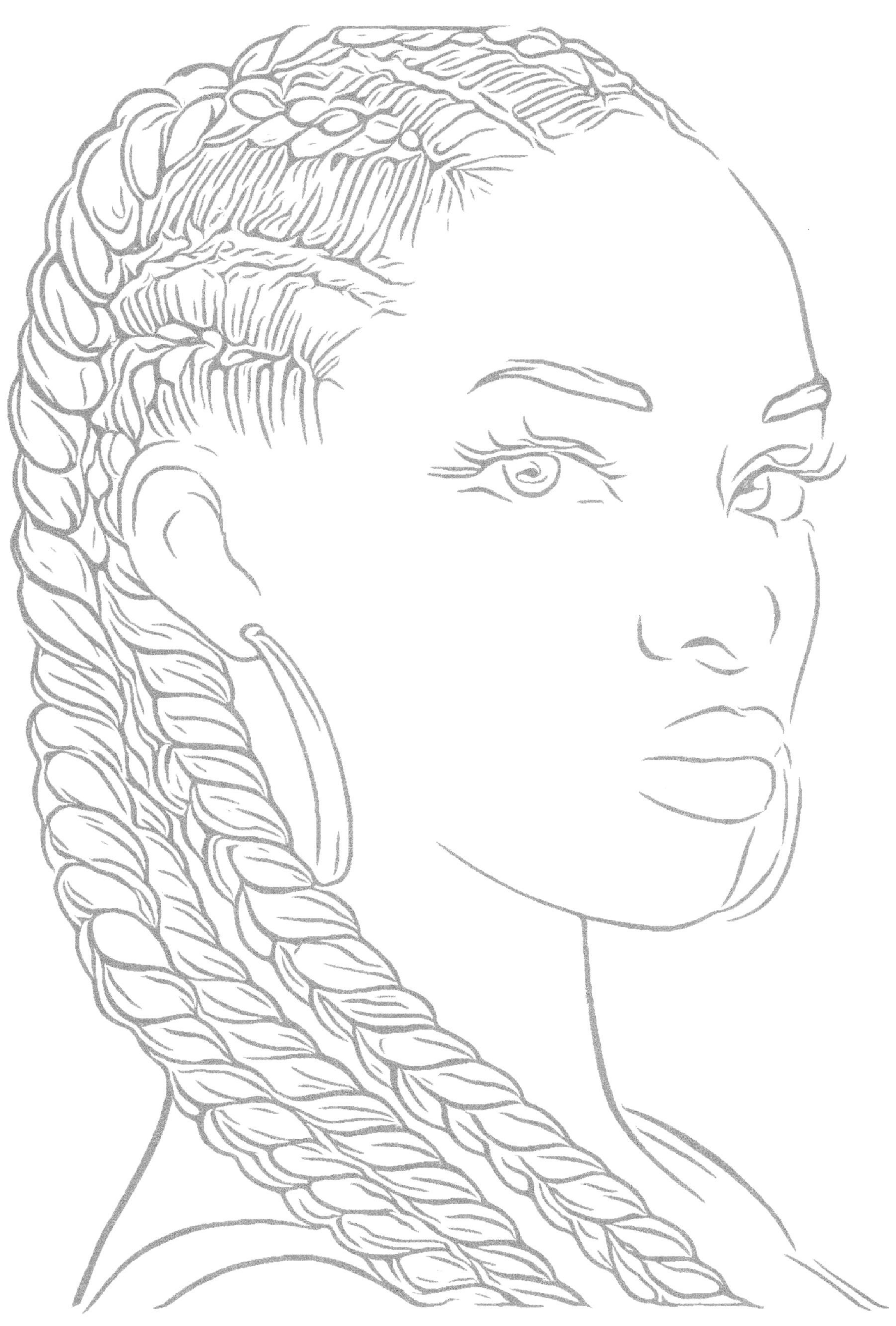

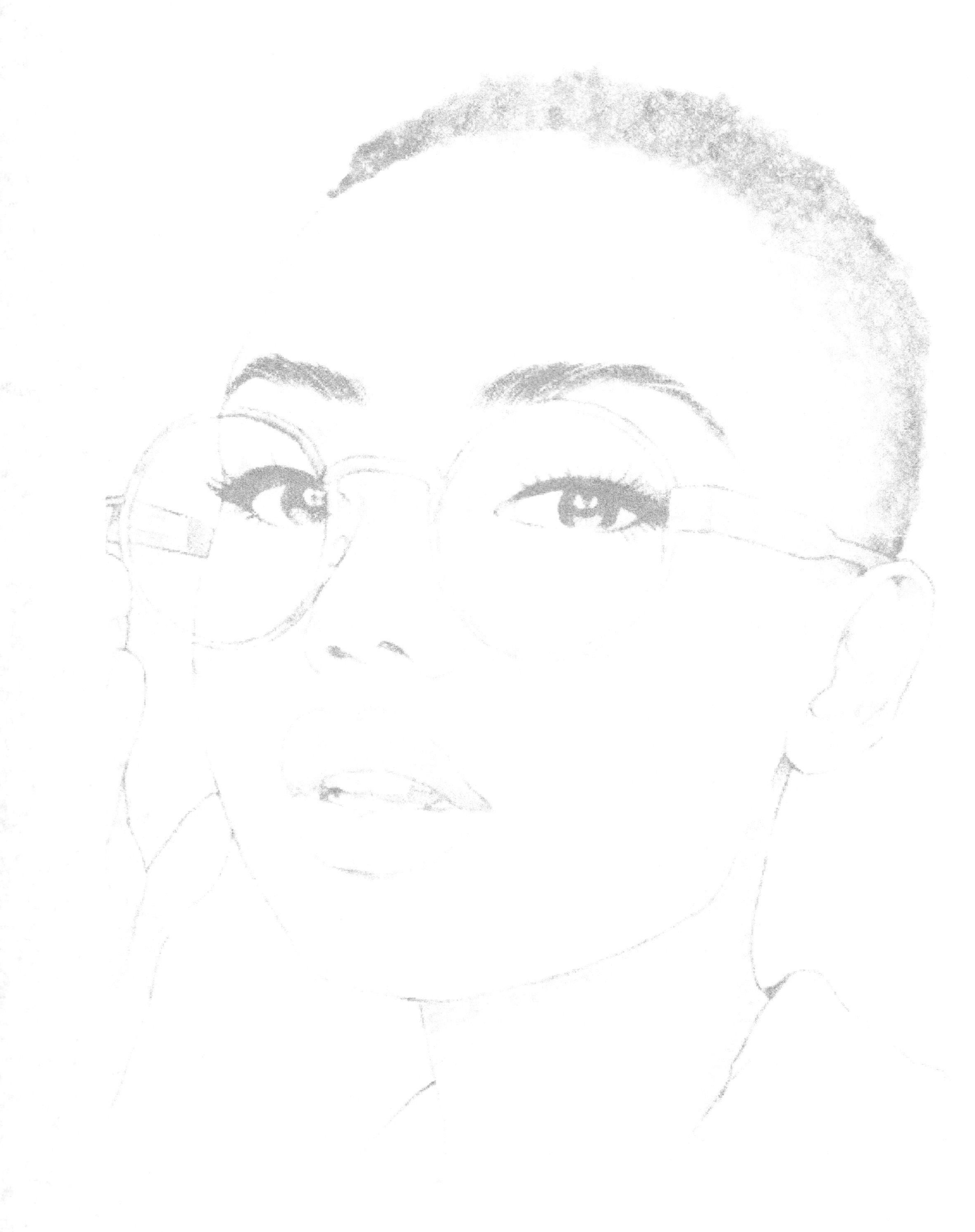

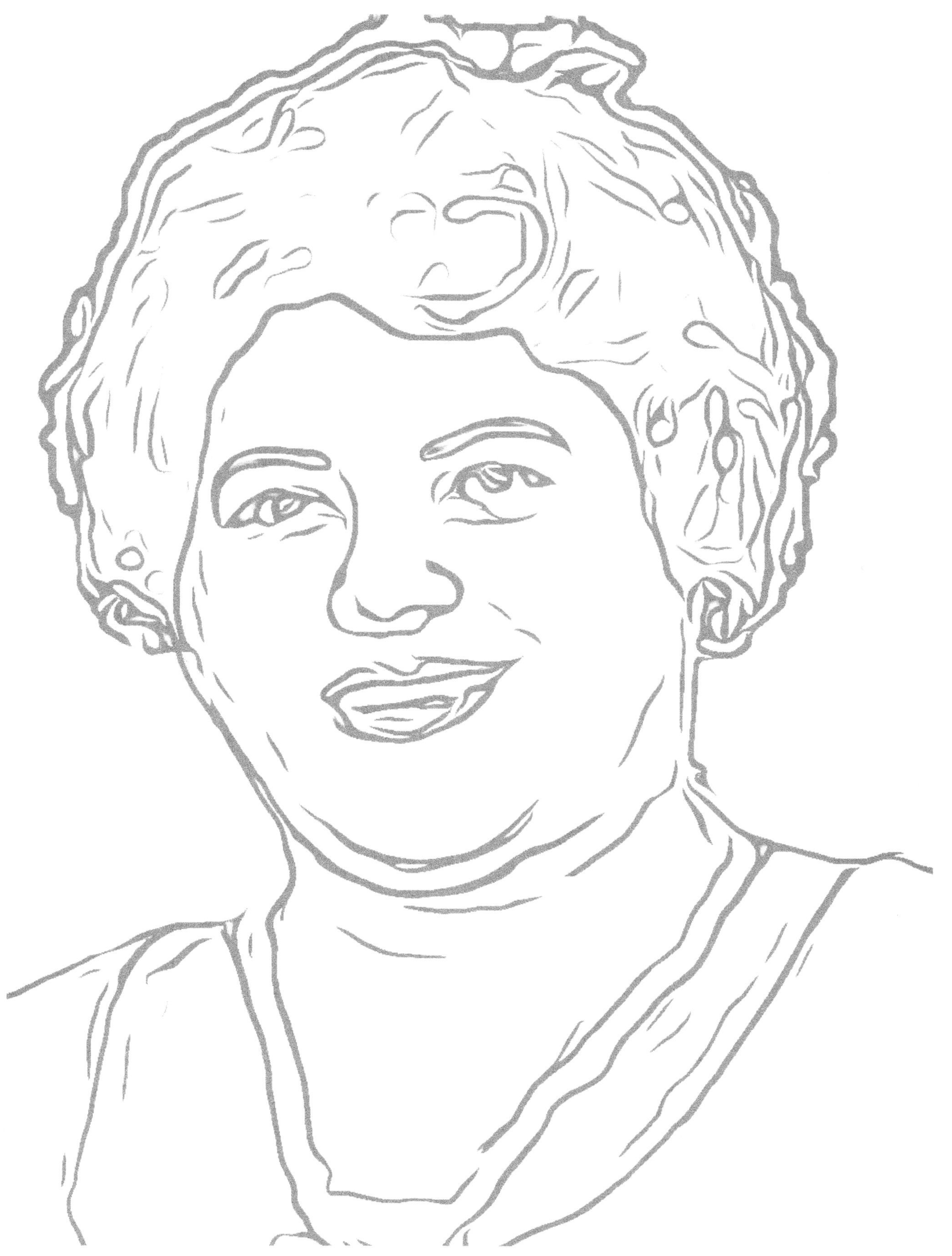

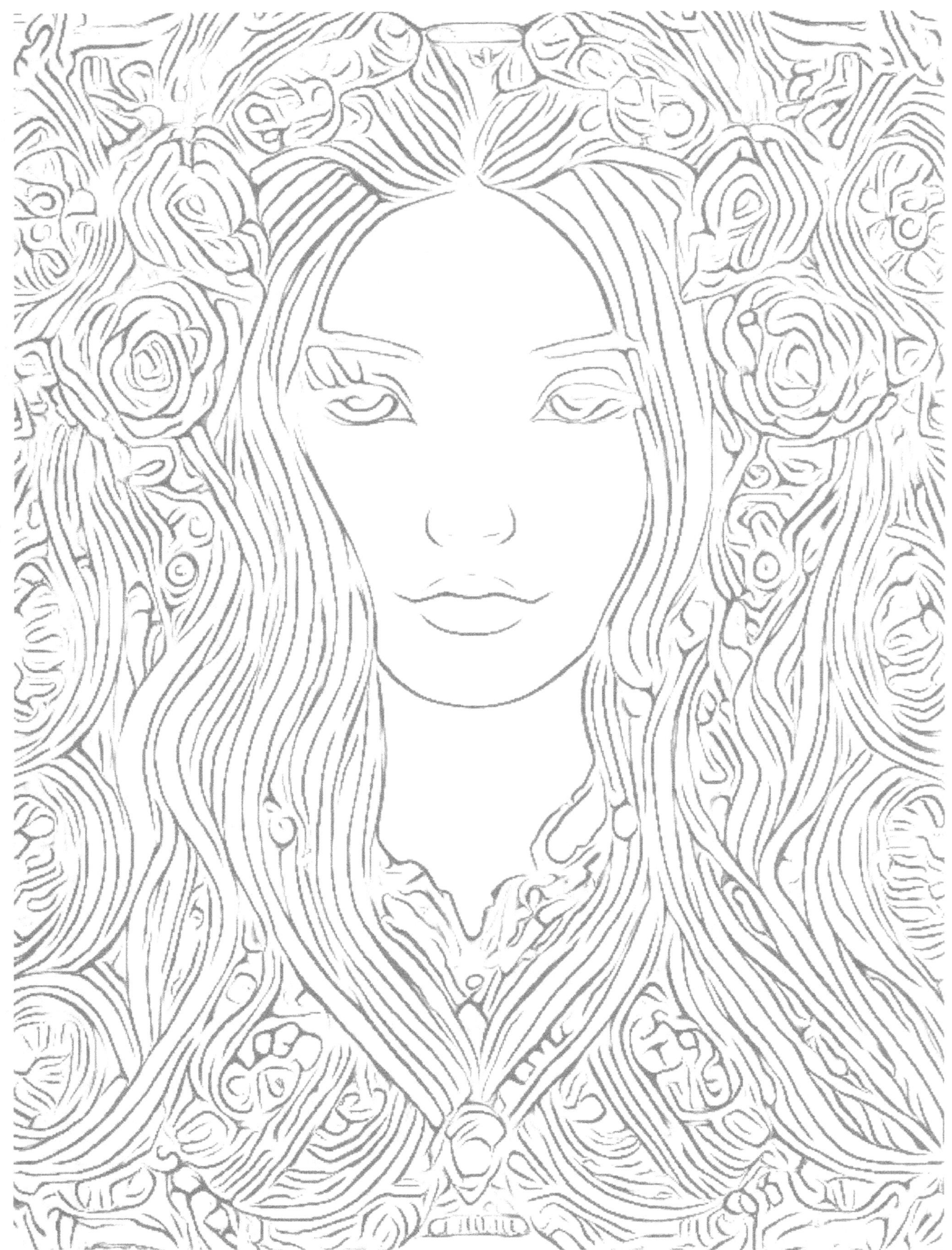

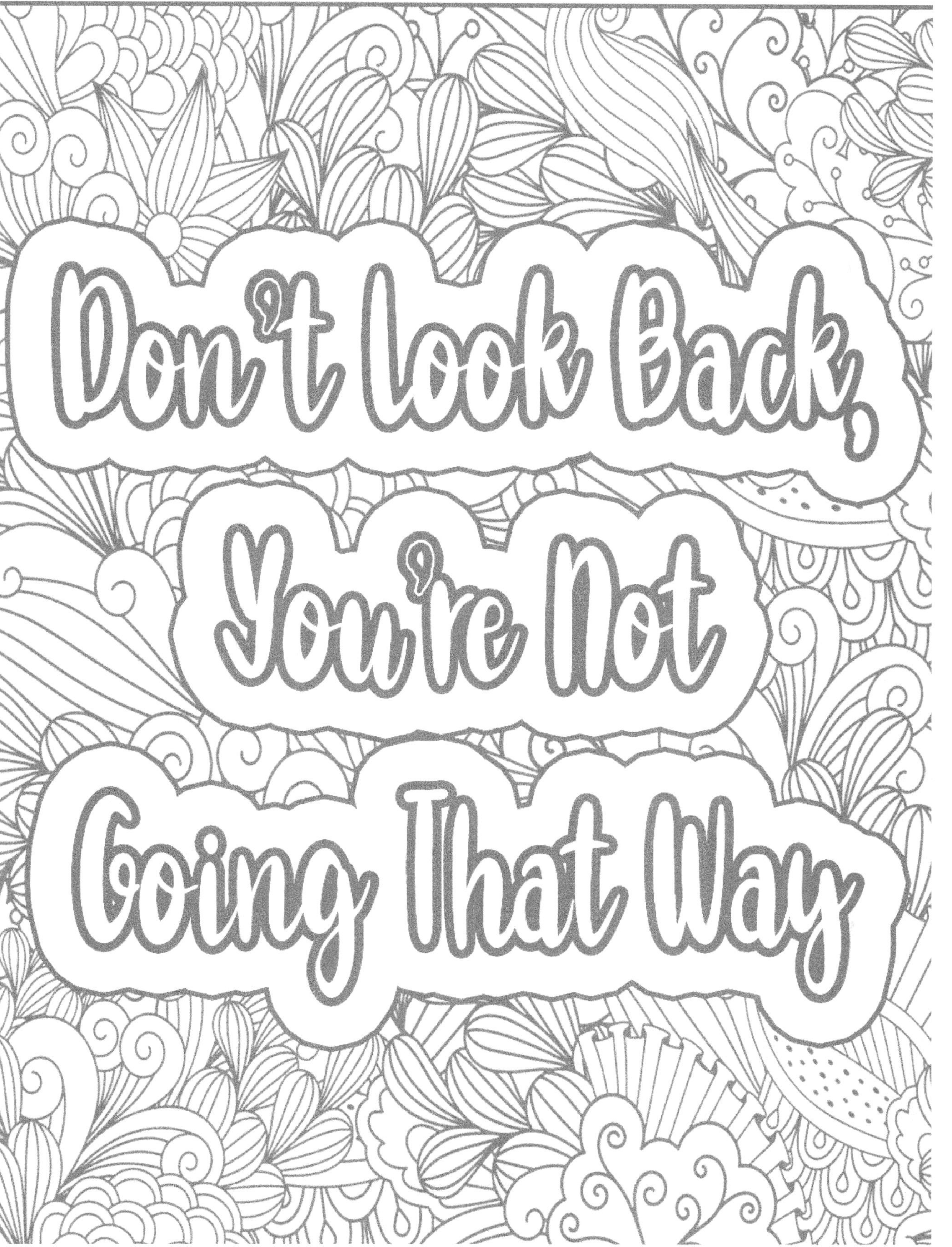

Don't look Back,
You're Not
Going That Way

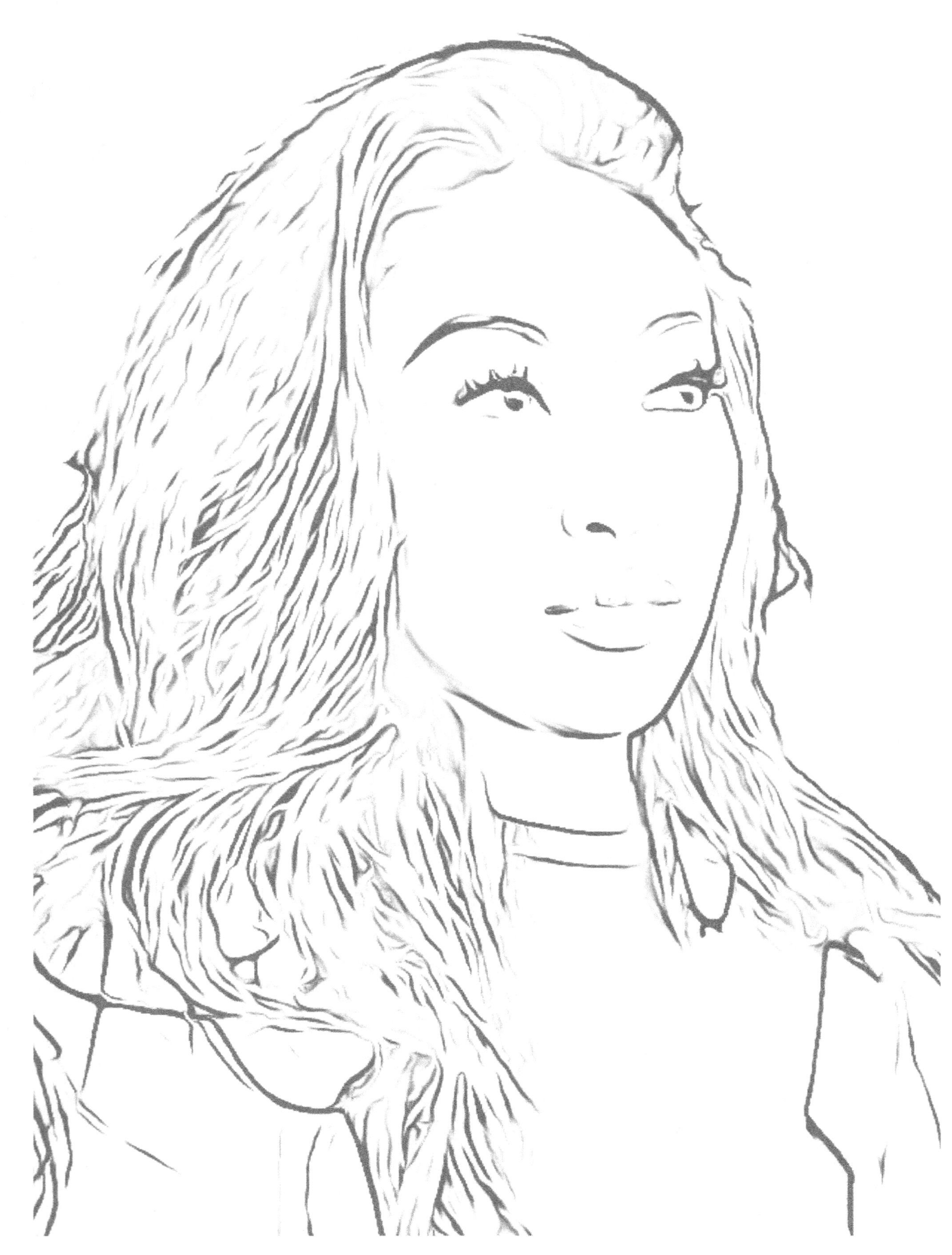

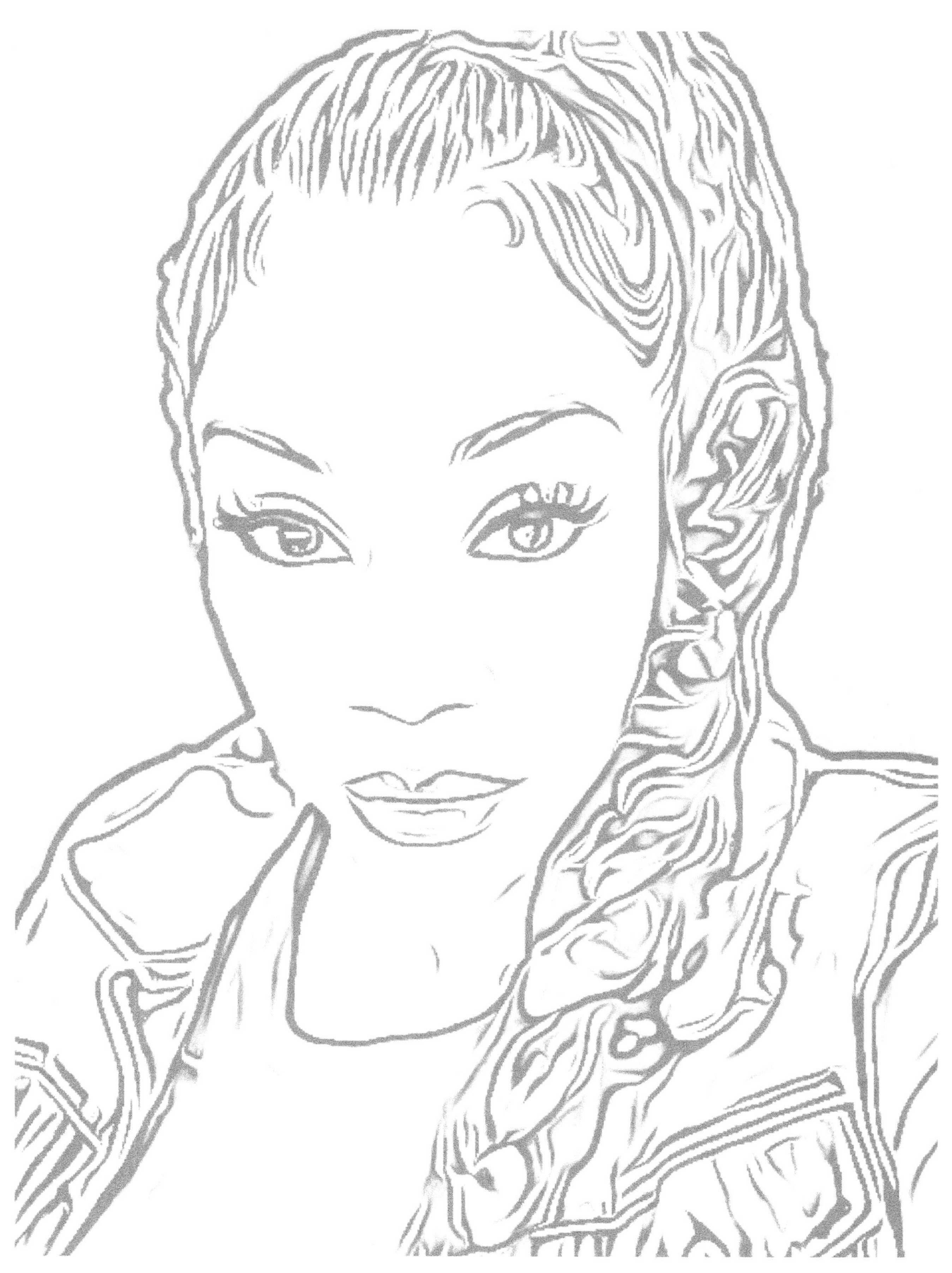

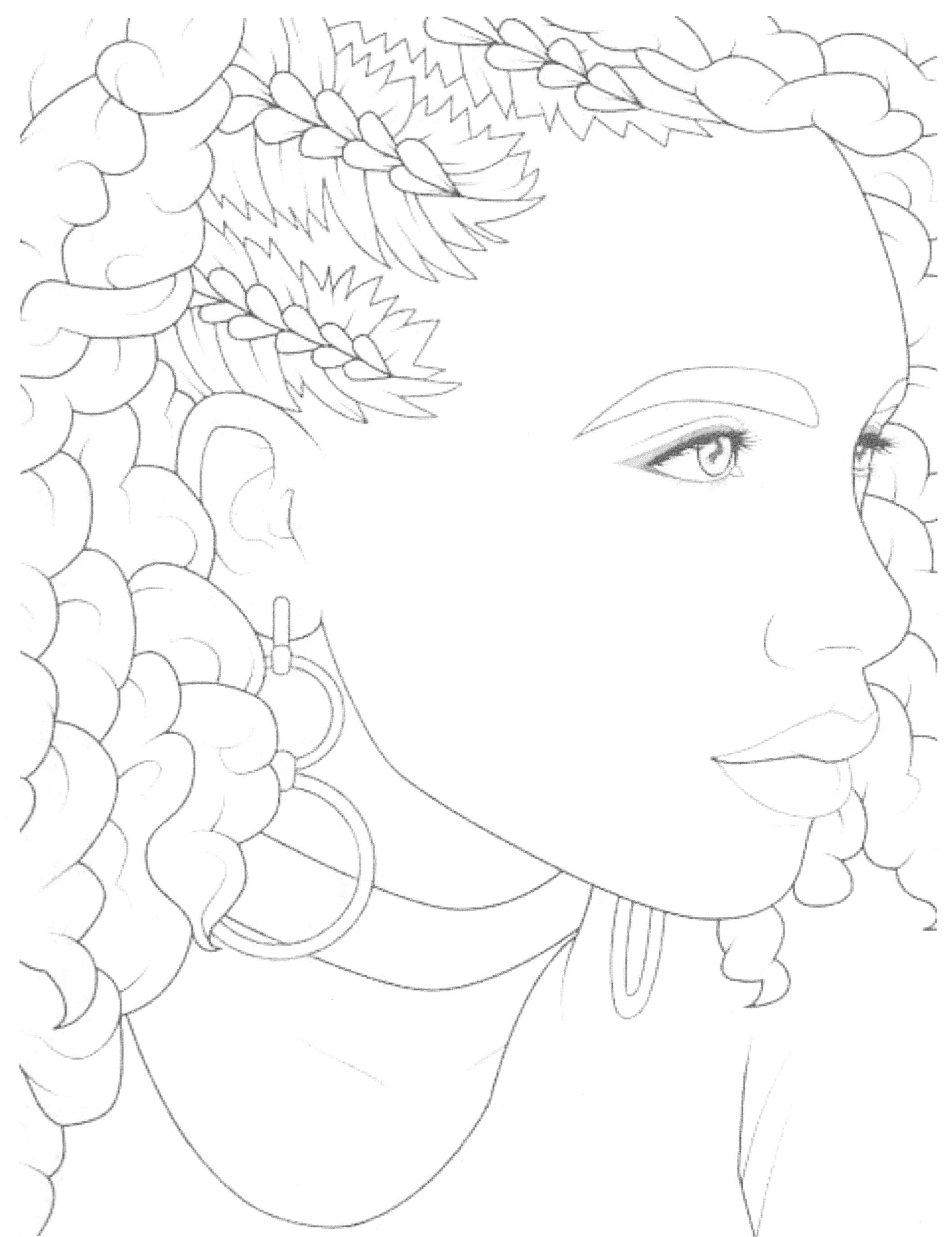

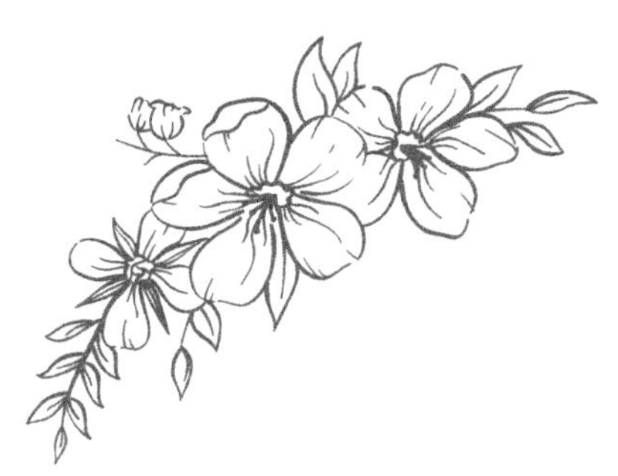

WITH AN OPEN
MIND AND
WILLING HEART,
I APPROACH
EACH DAY AS
A NEW
OPPORTUNITY.

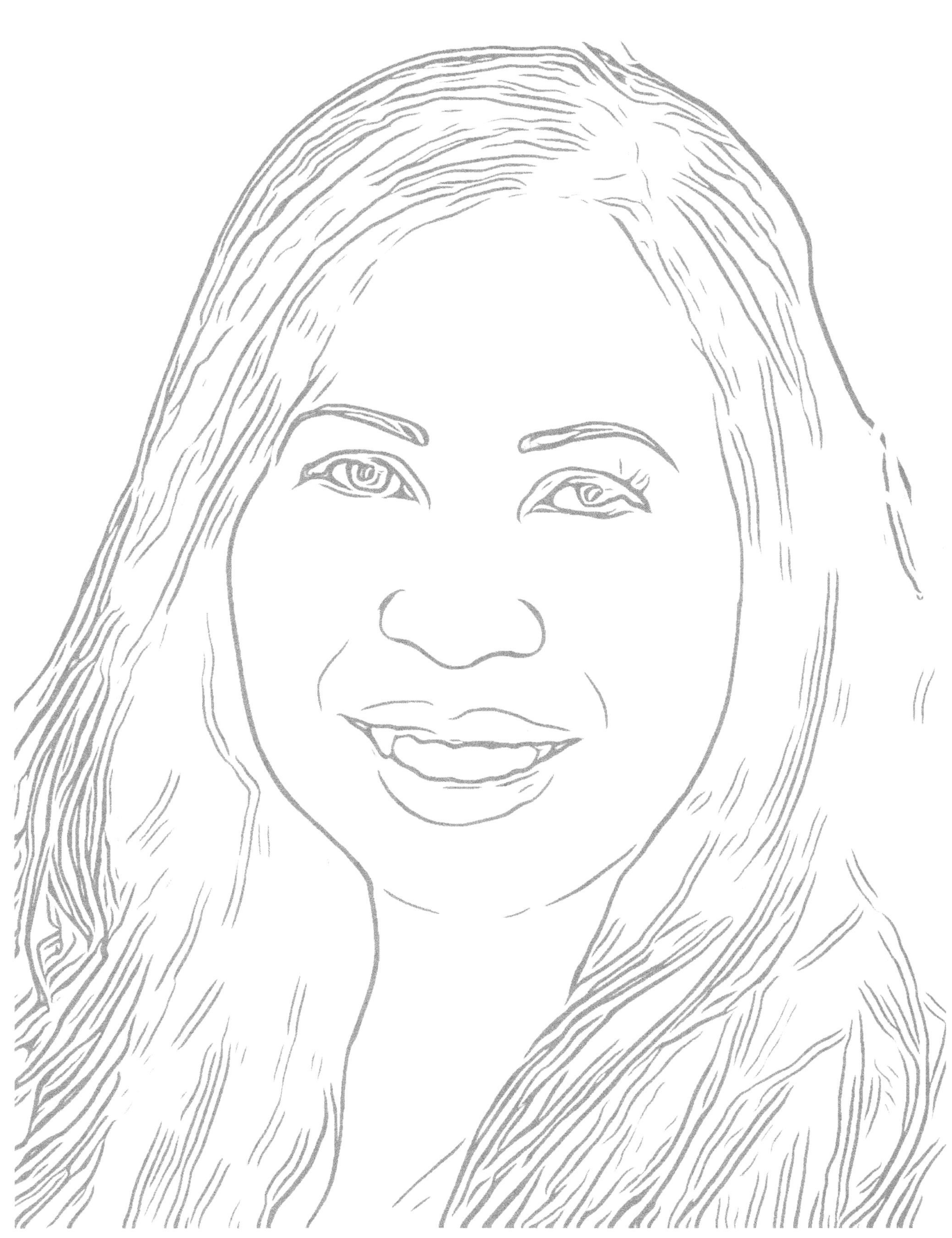

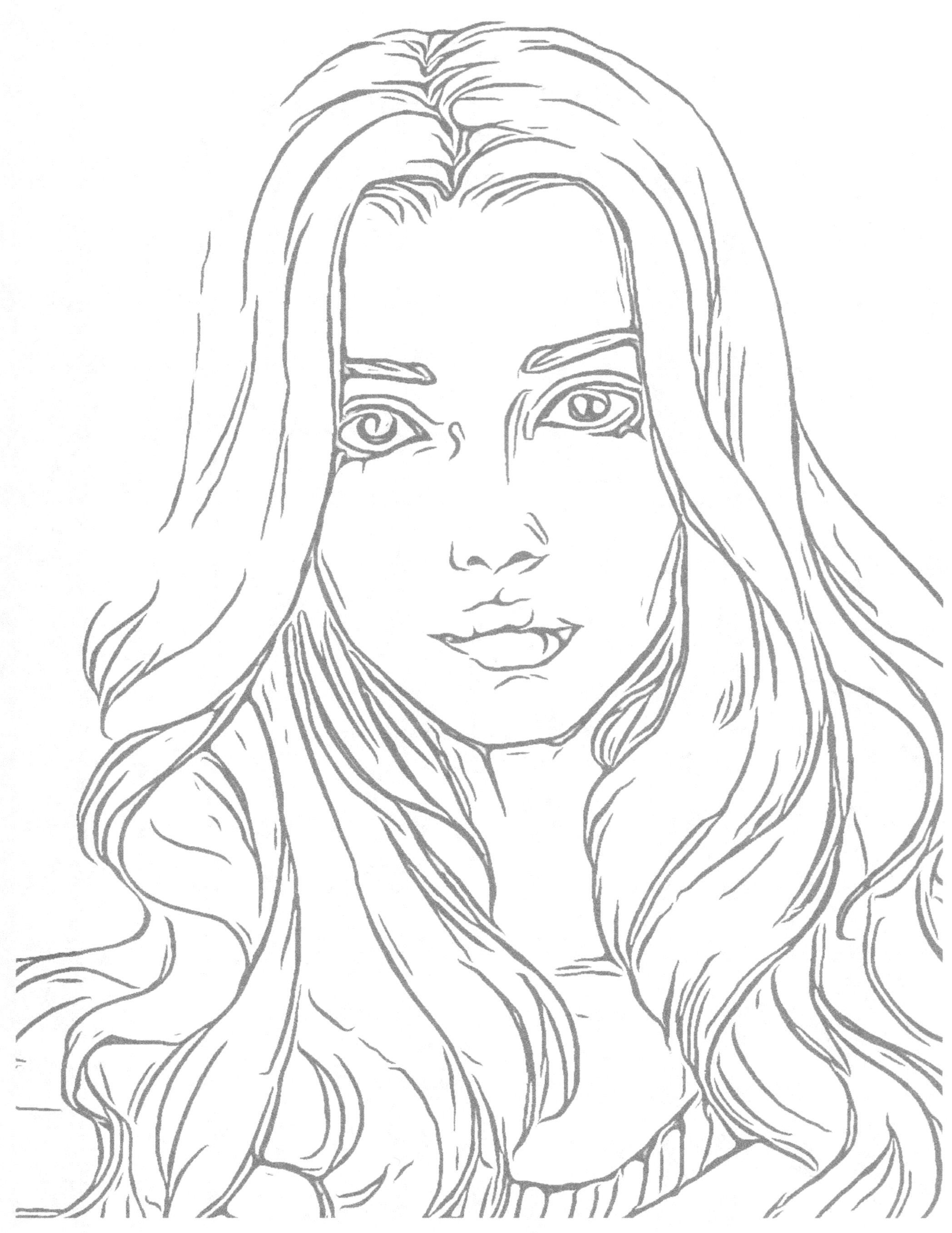

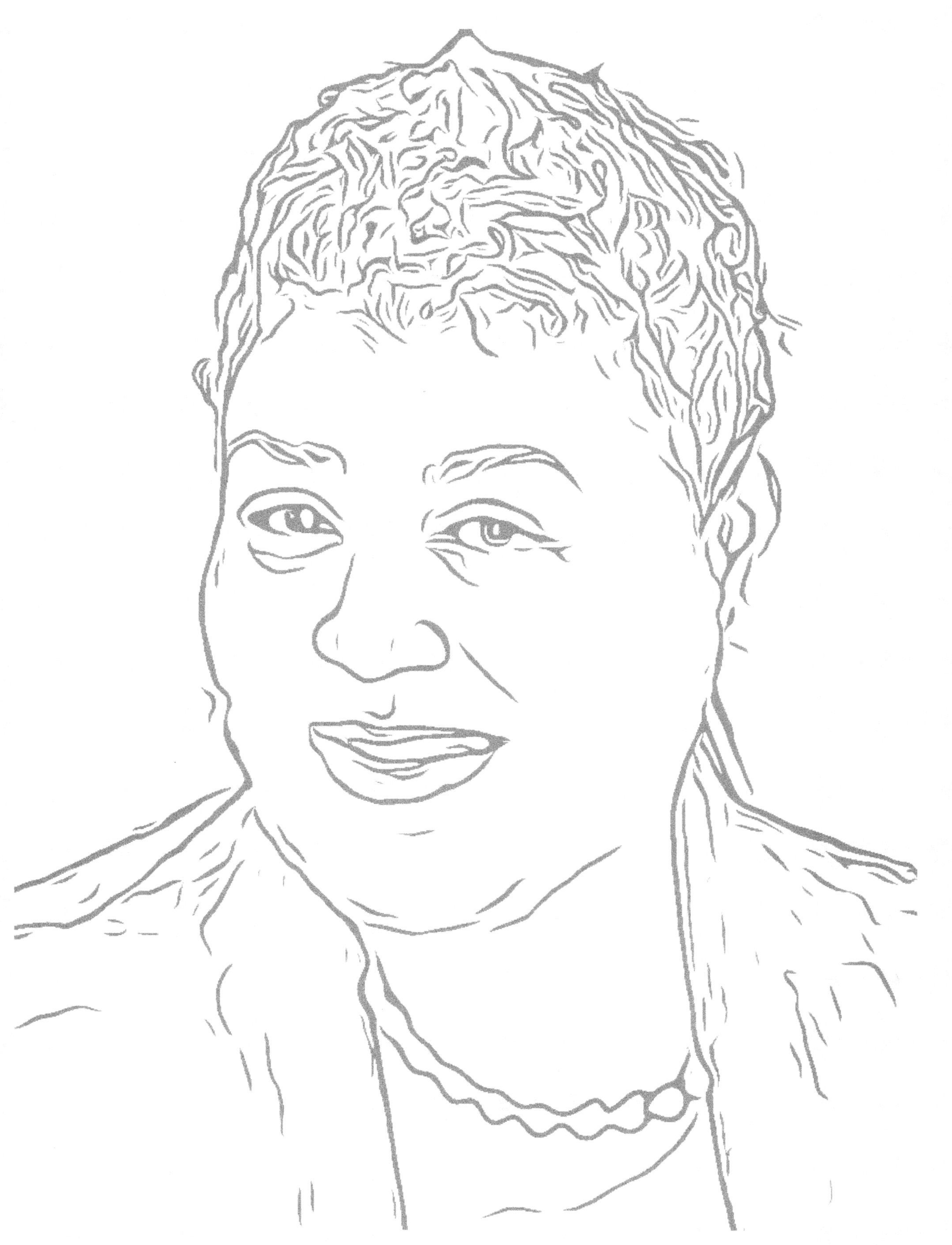

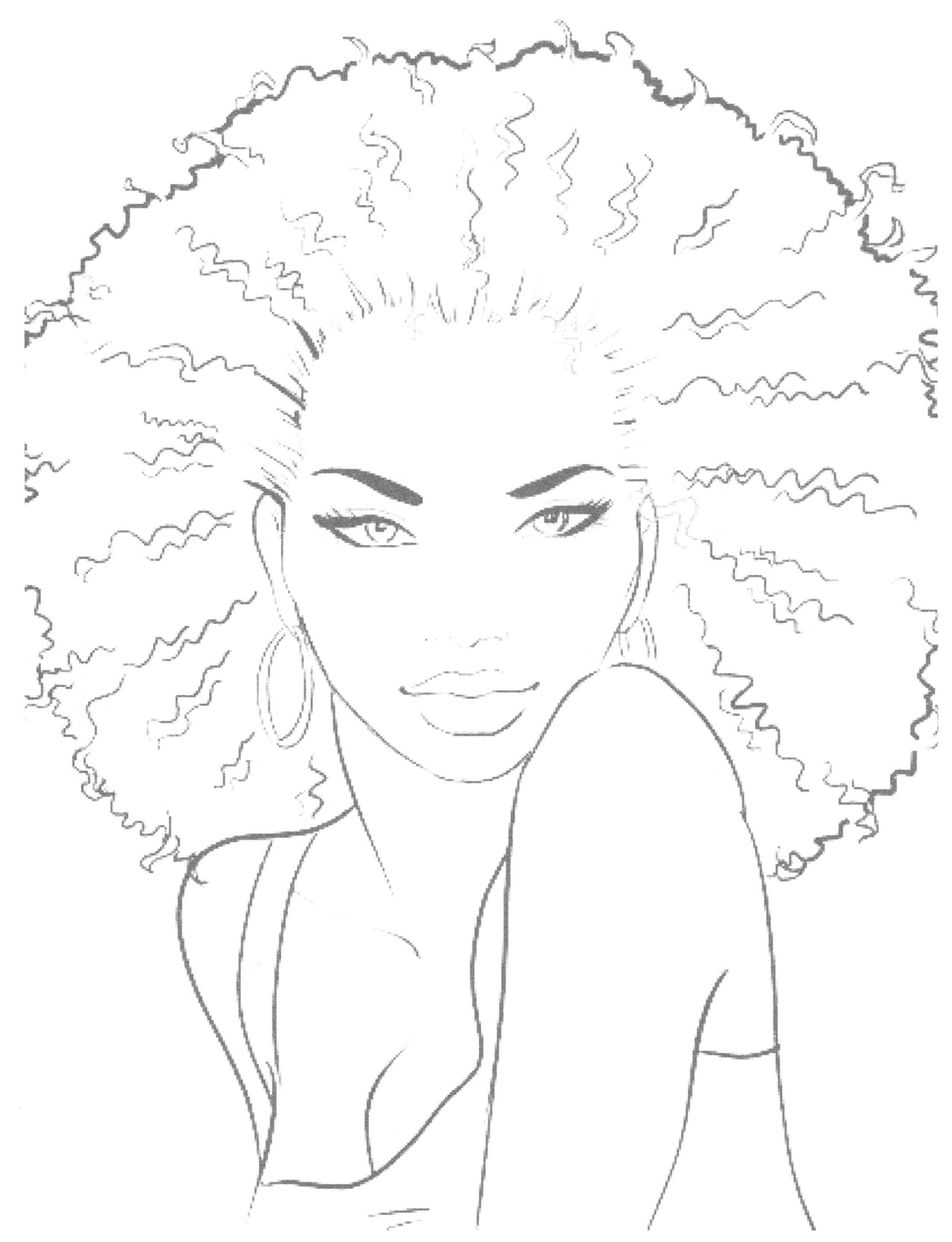

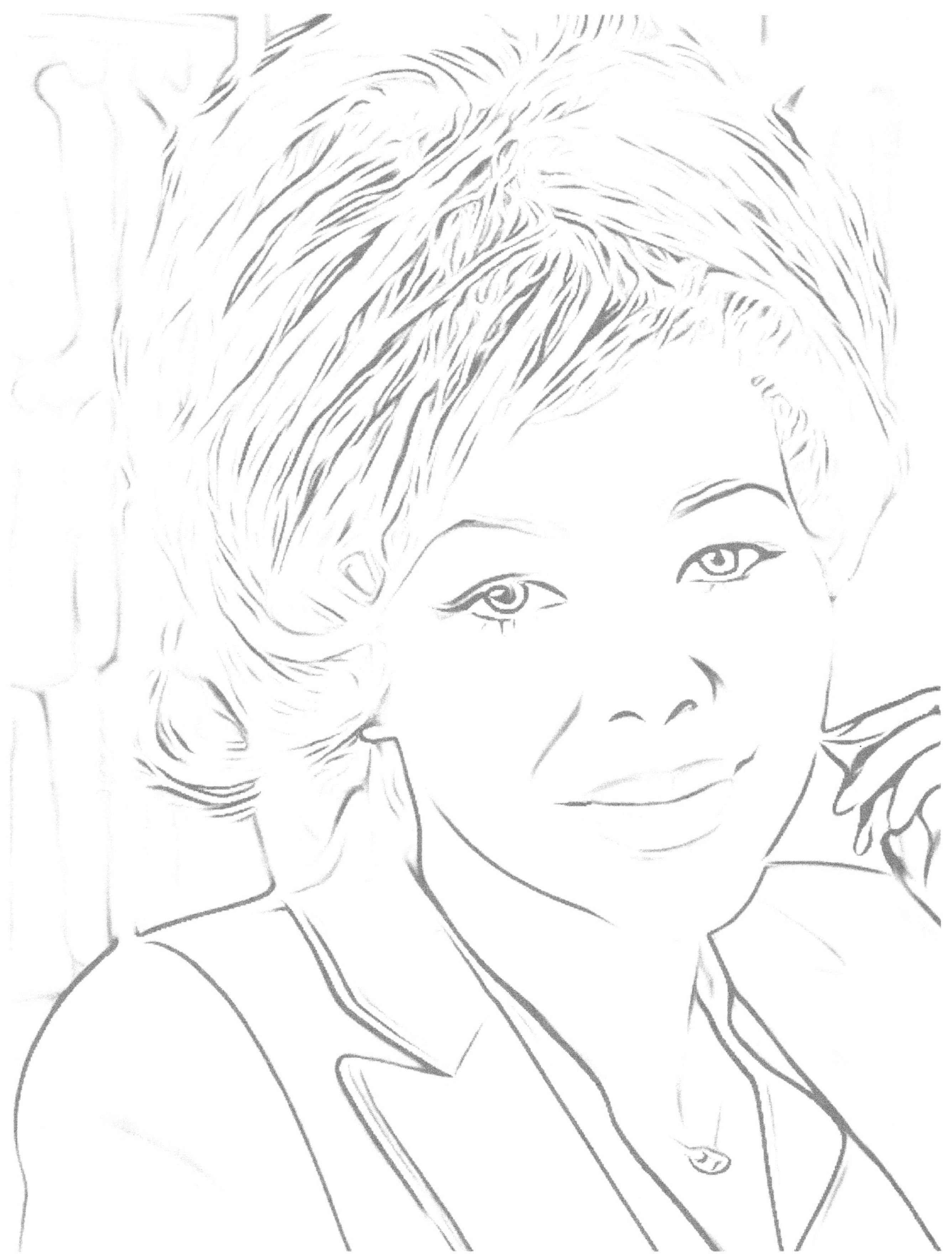

# I AM A STRONG AND CONFIDENT WOMAN.

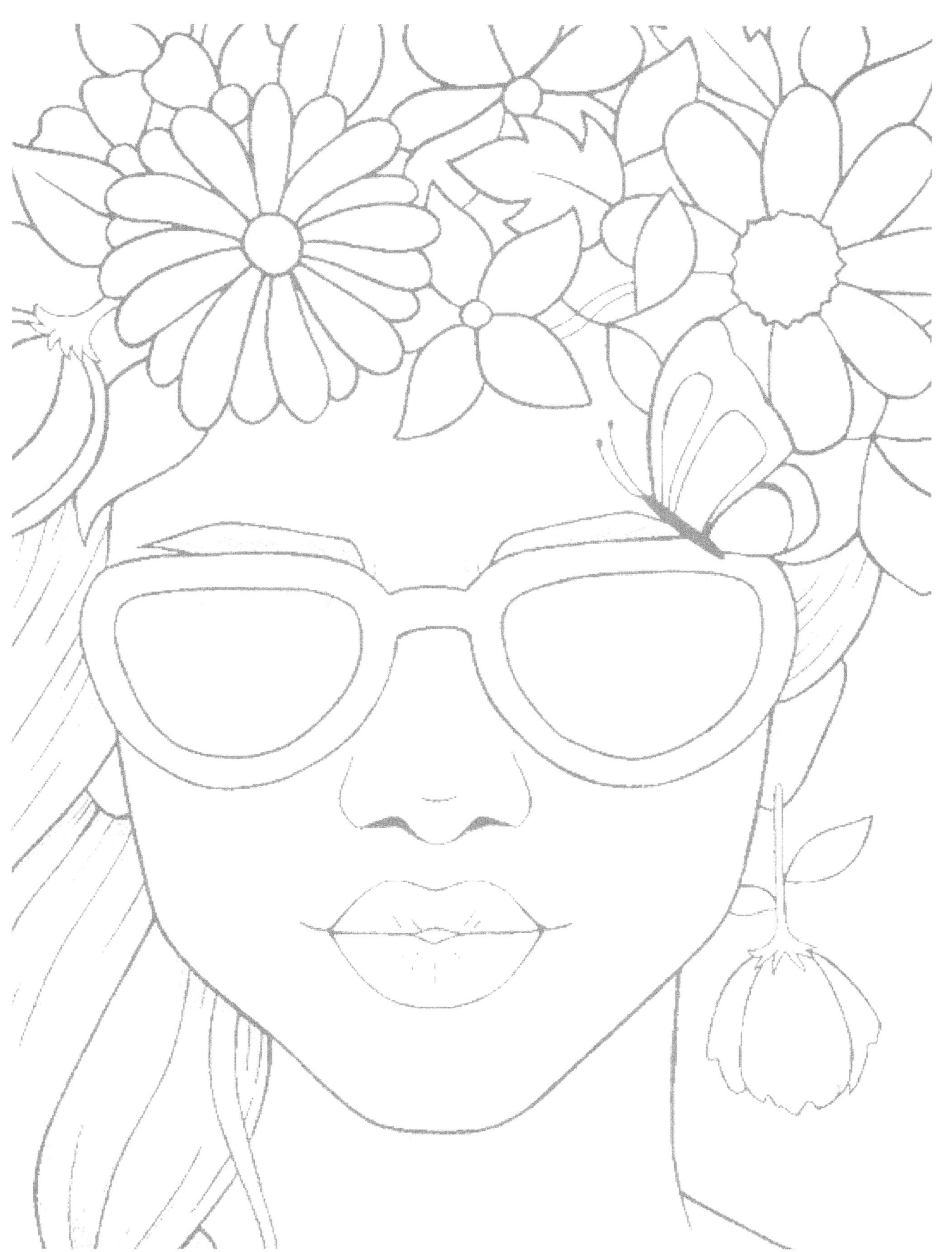

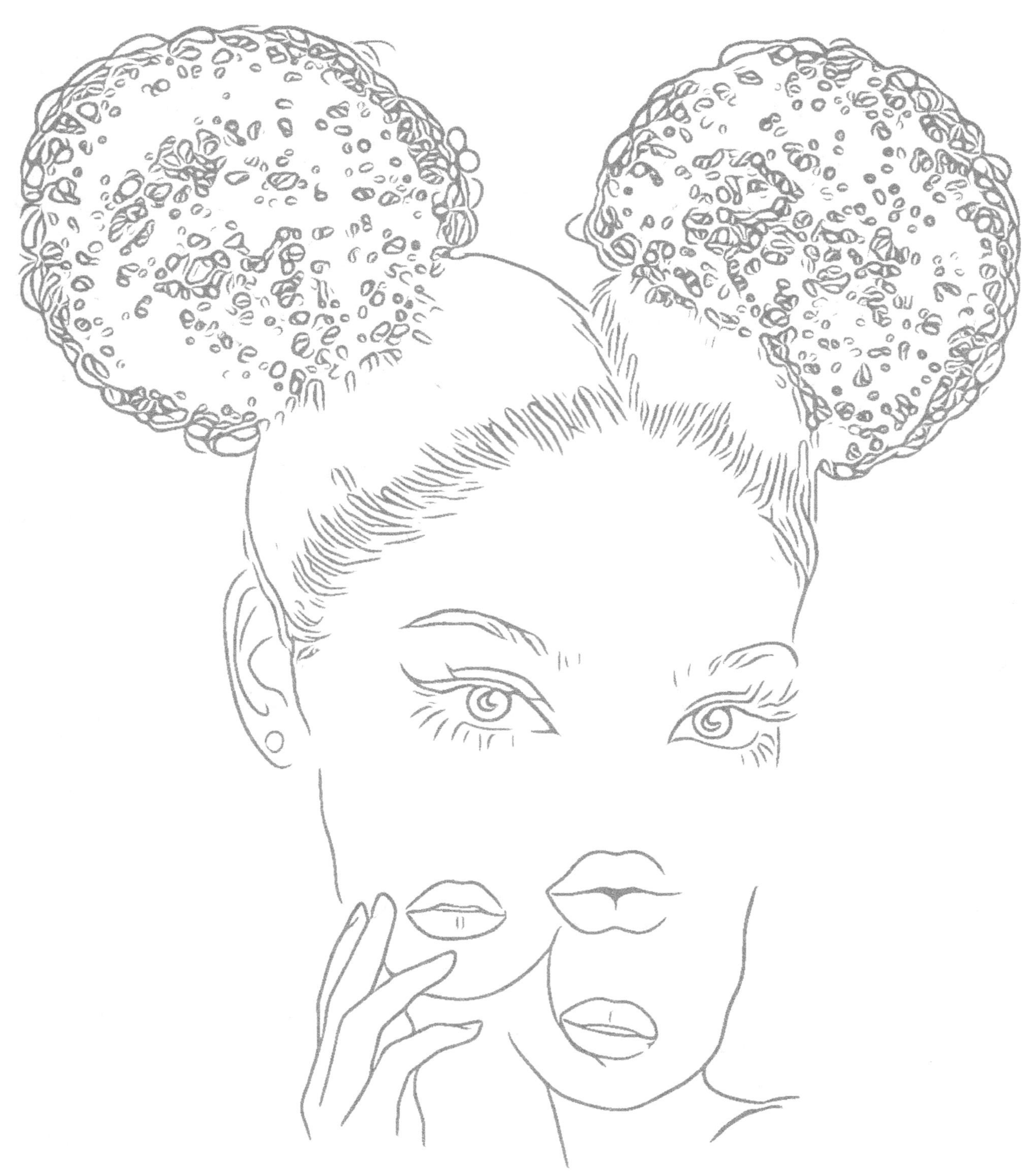

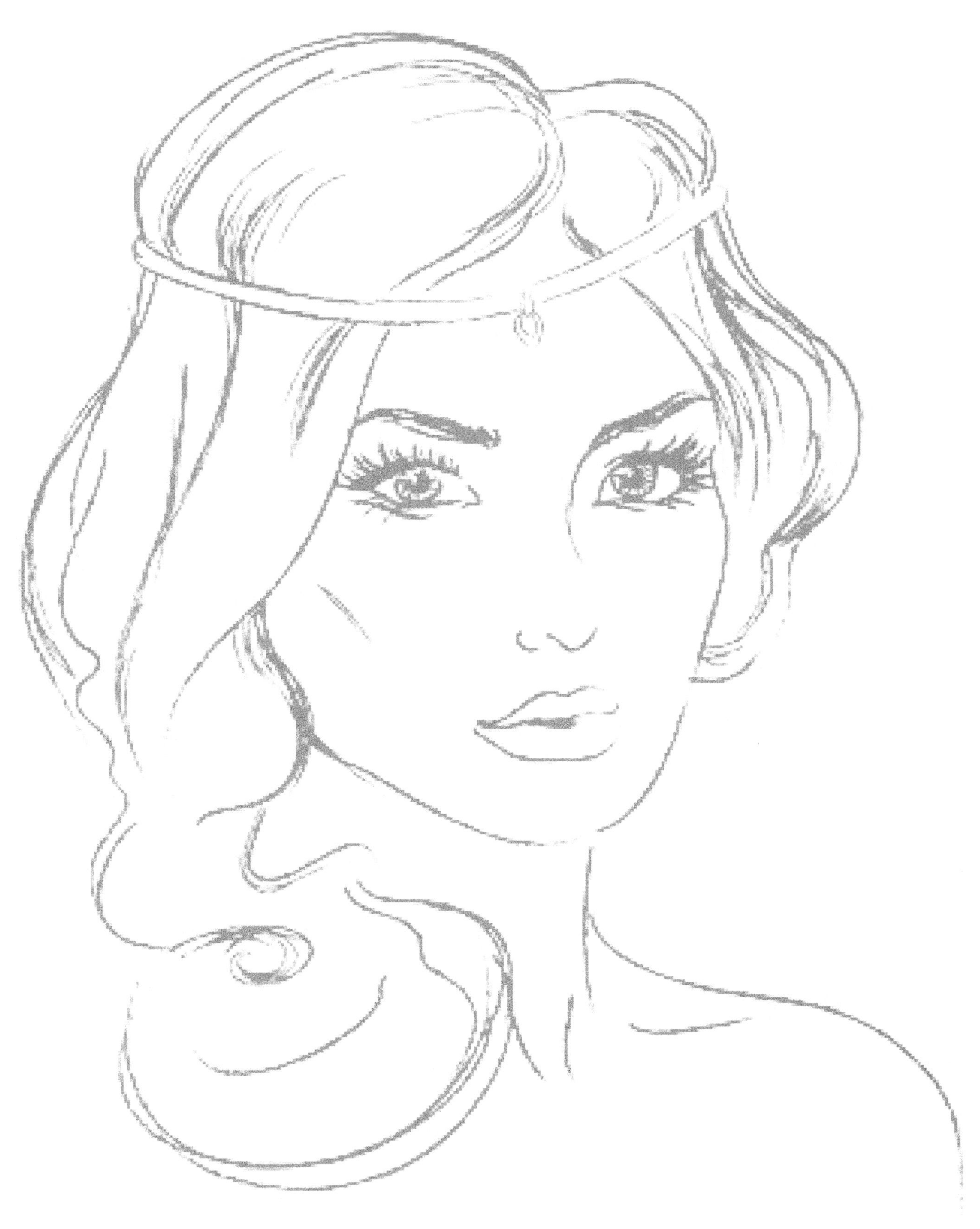

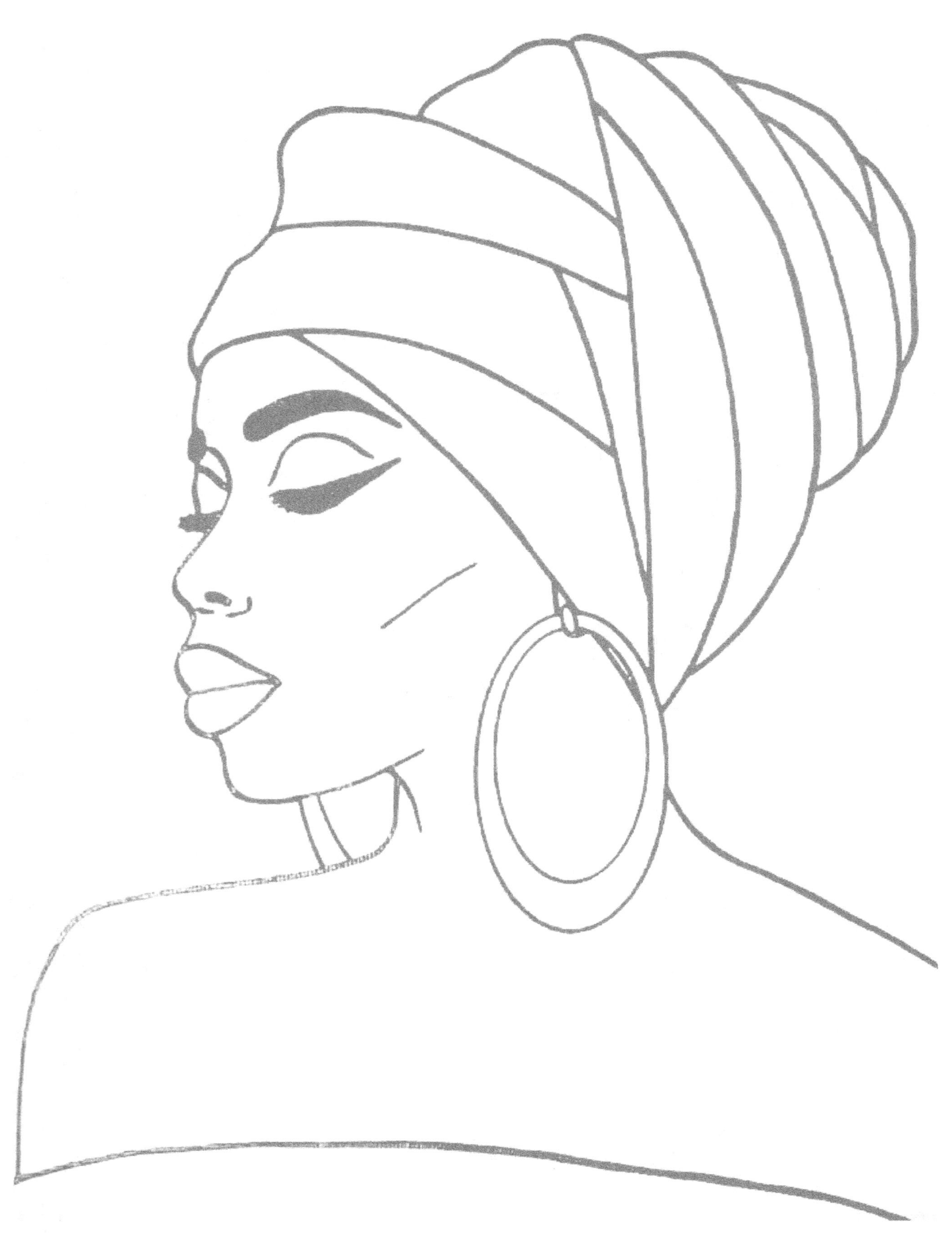

I AM ENOUGH

I AM ENOUGH

I AM ENOUGH

I AM ENOUGH

I AM ENOUGH

I AM ENOUGH

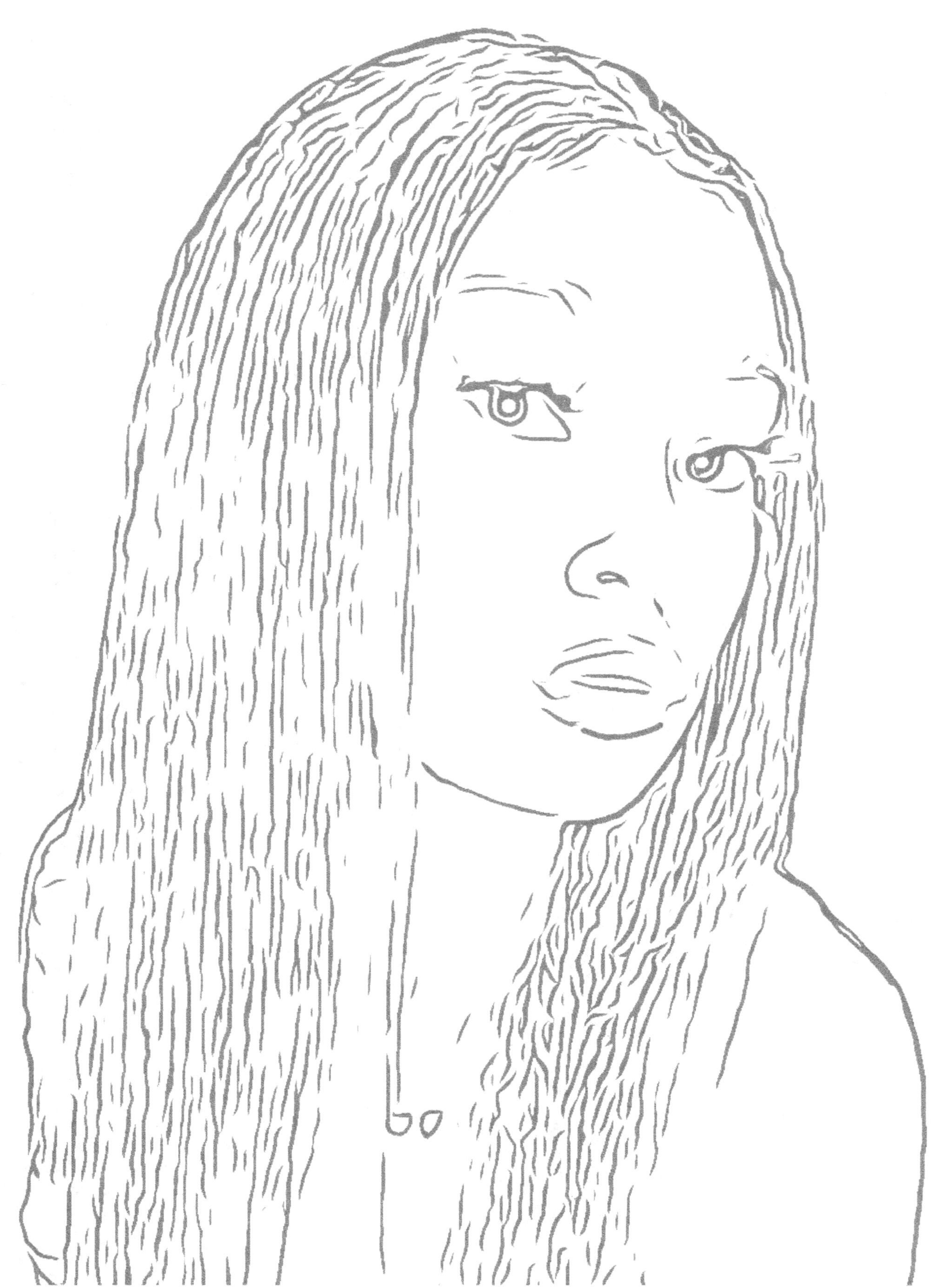

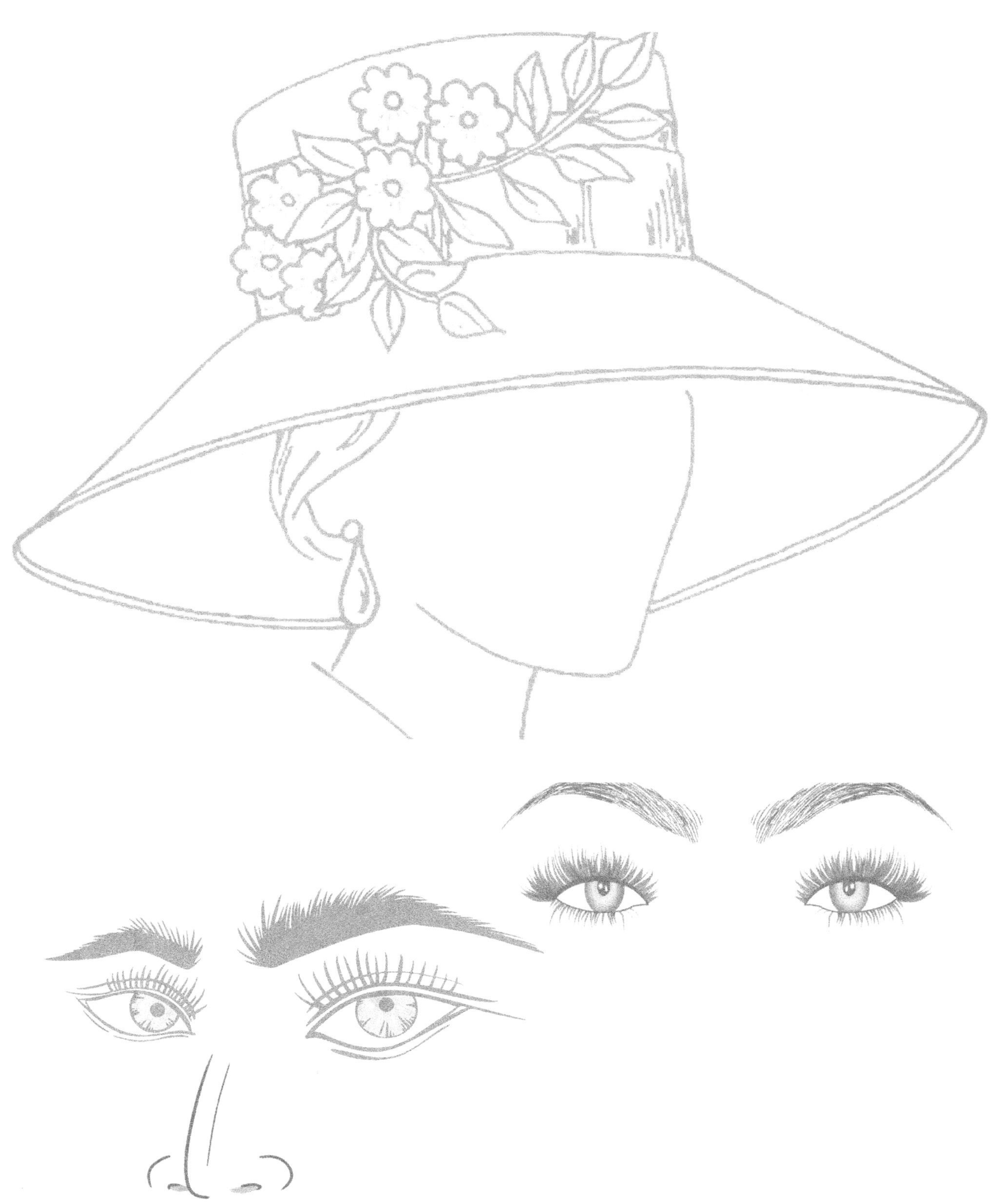

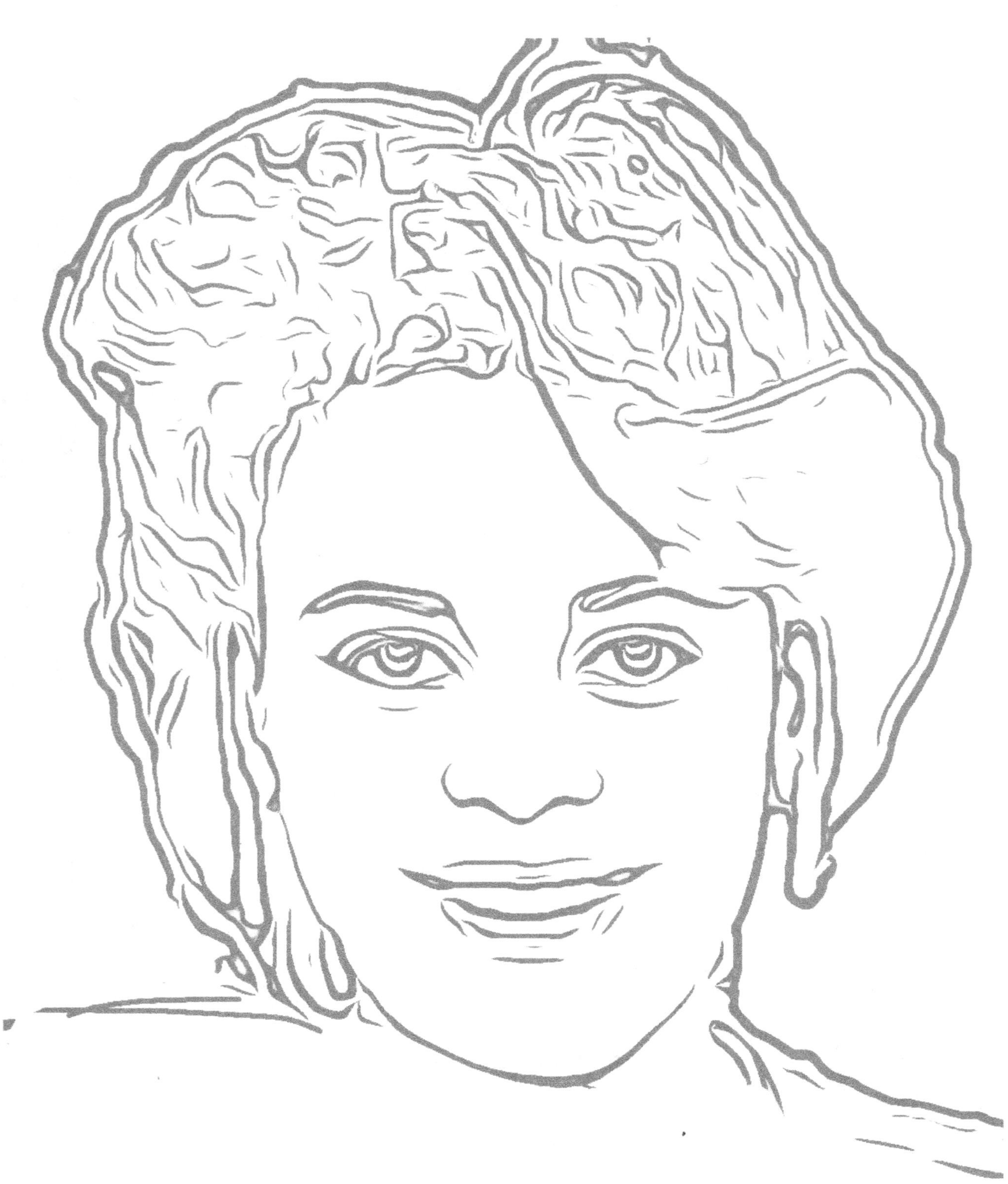

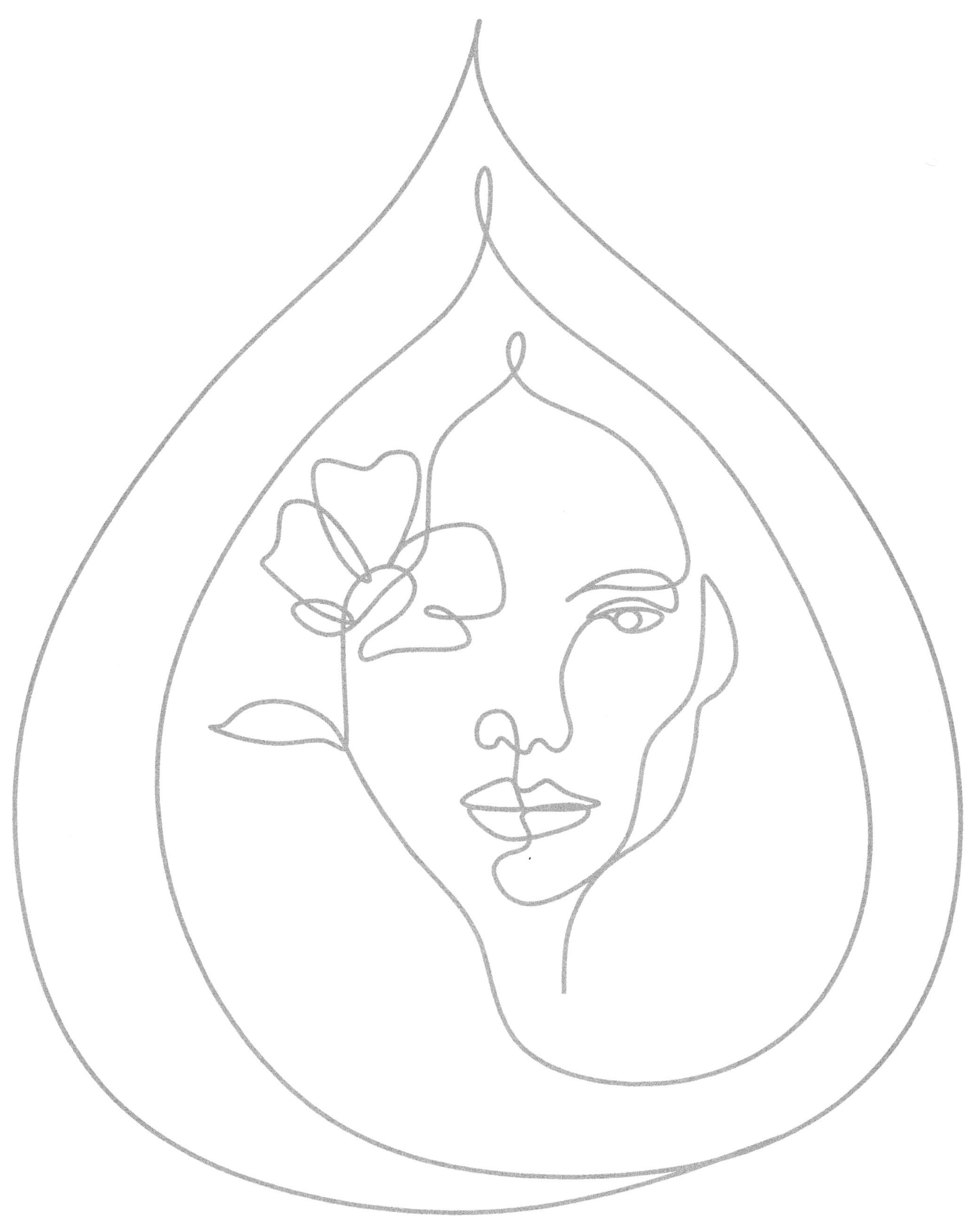

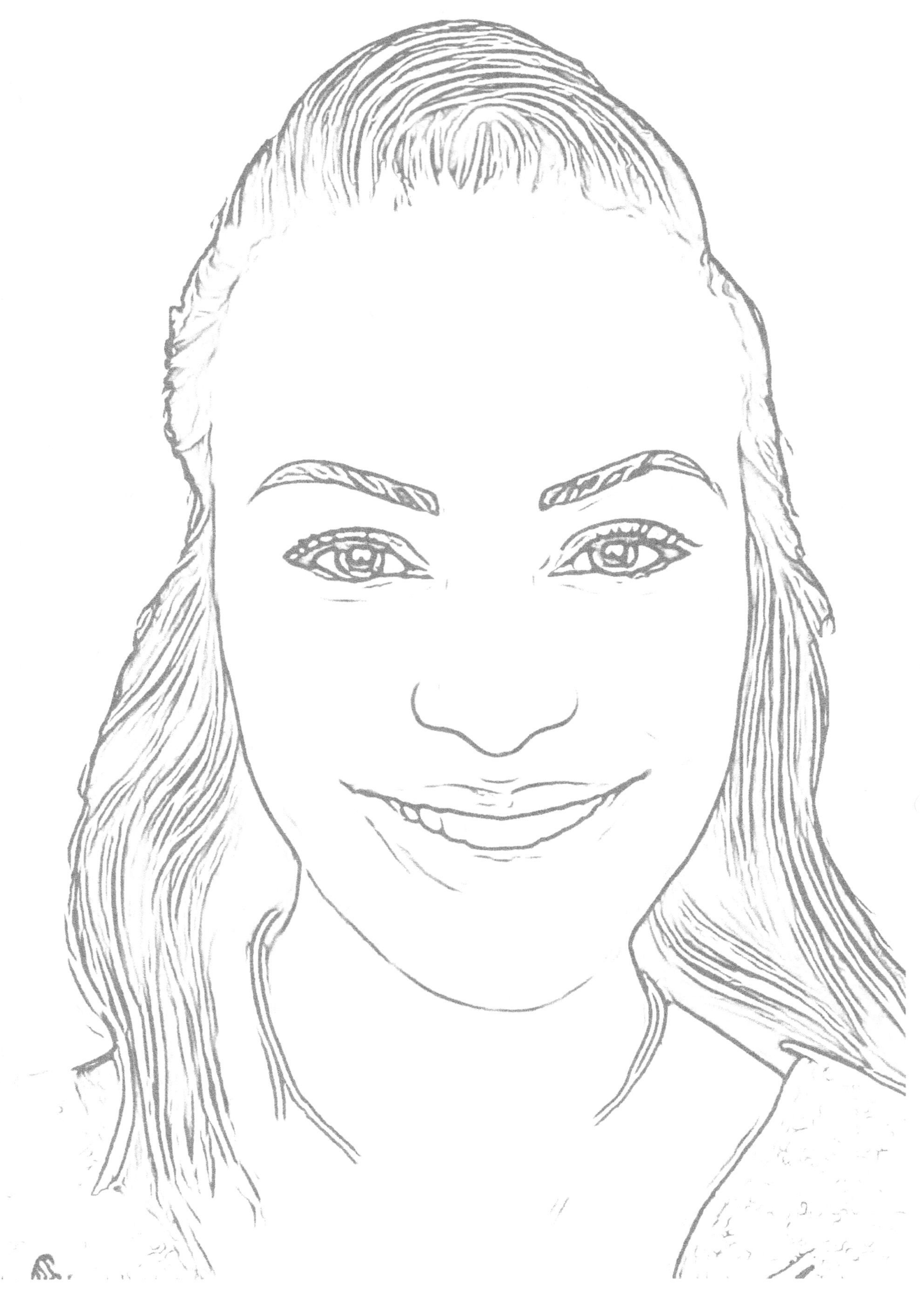

# MY HEART IS FULL OF LOVE FOR MYSELF.

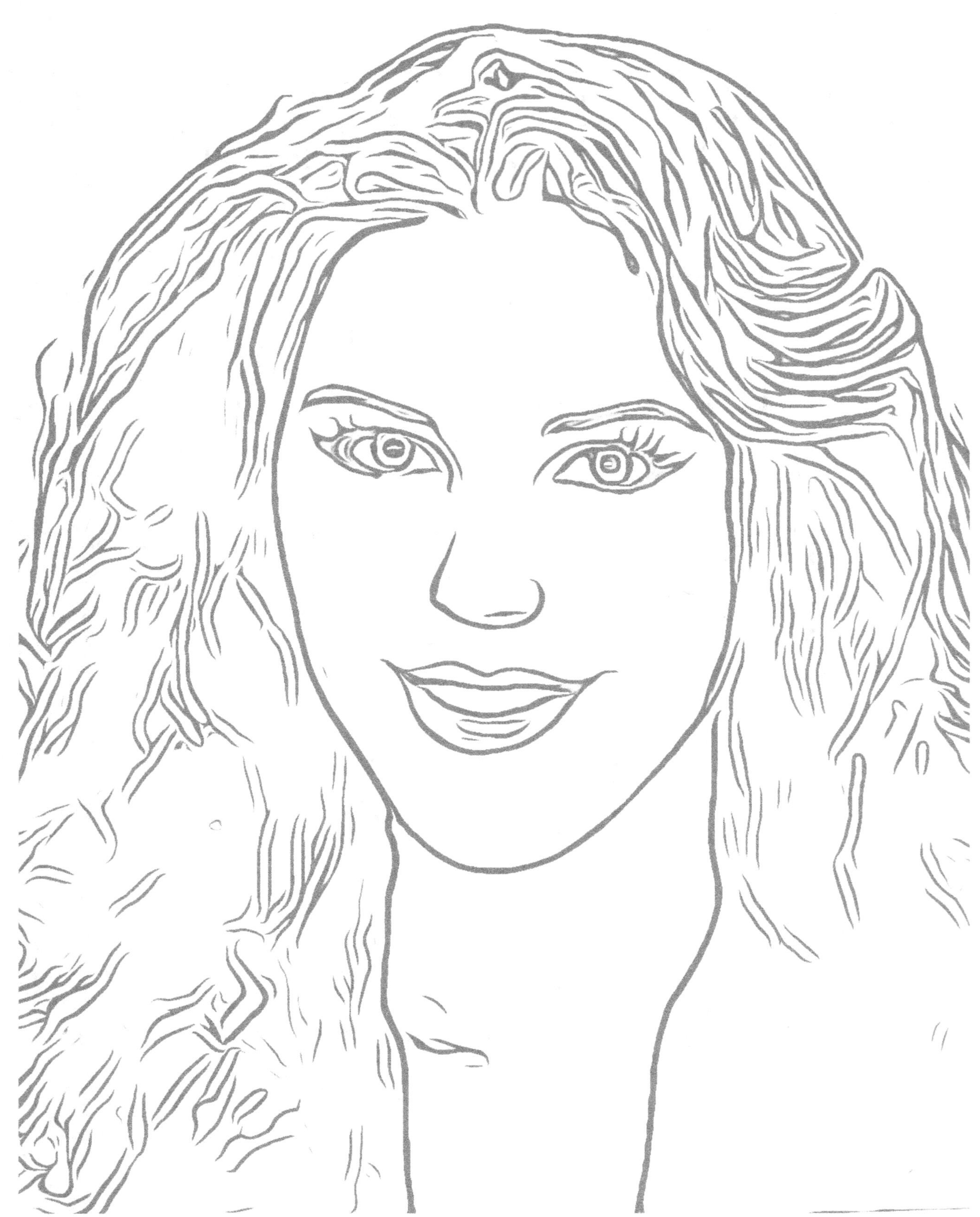

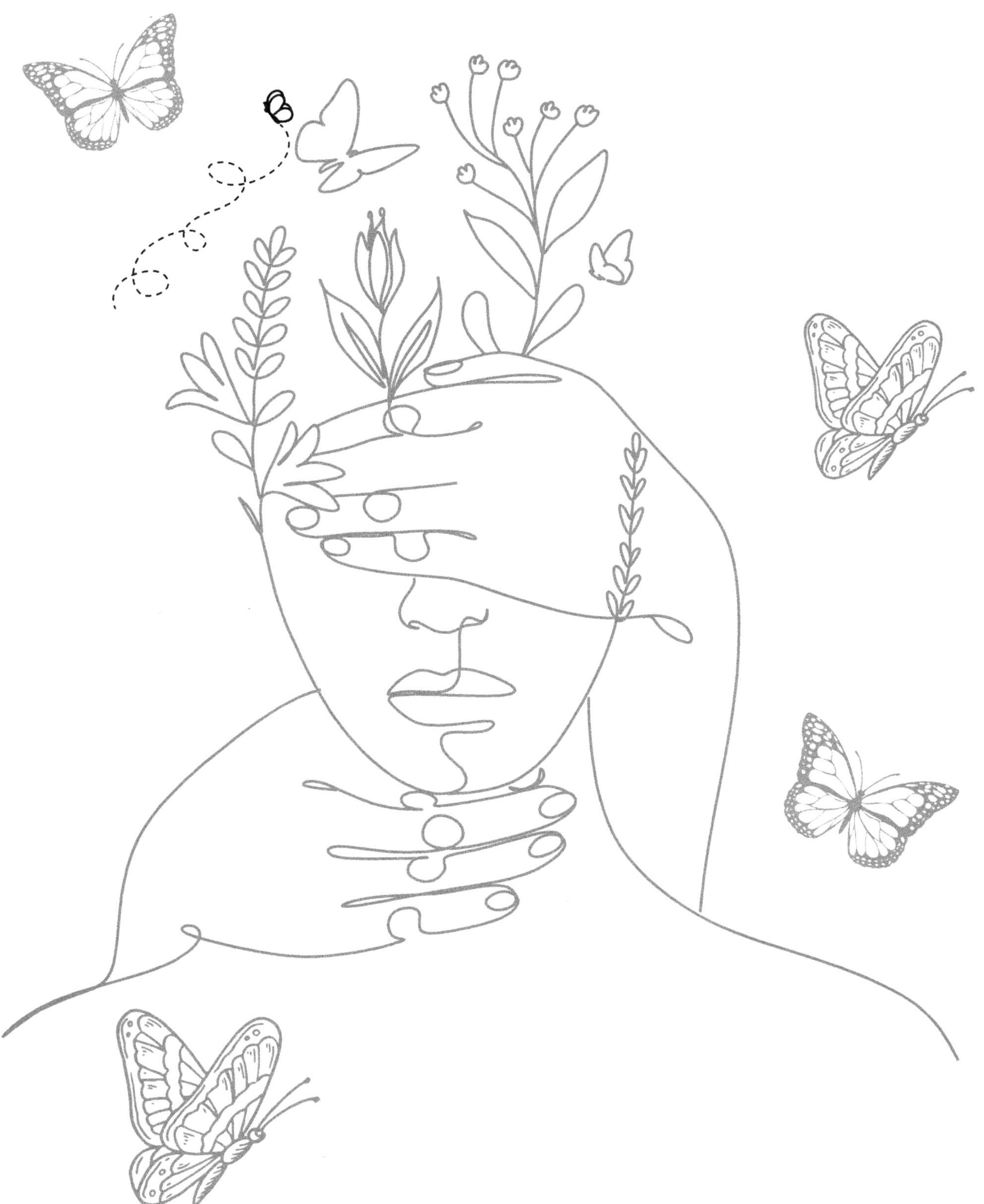

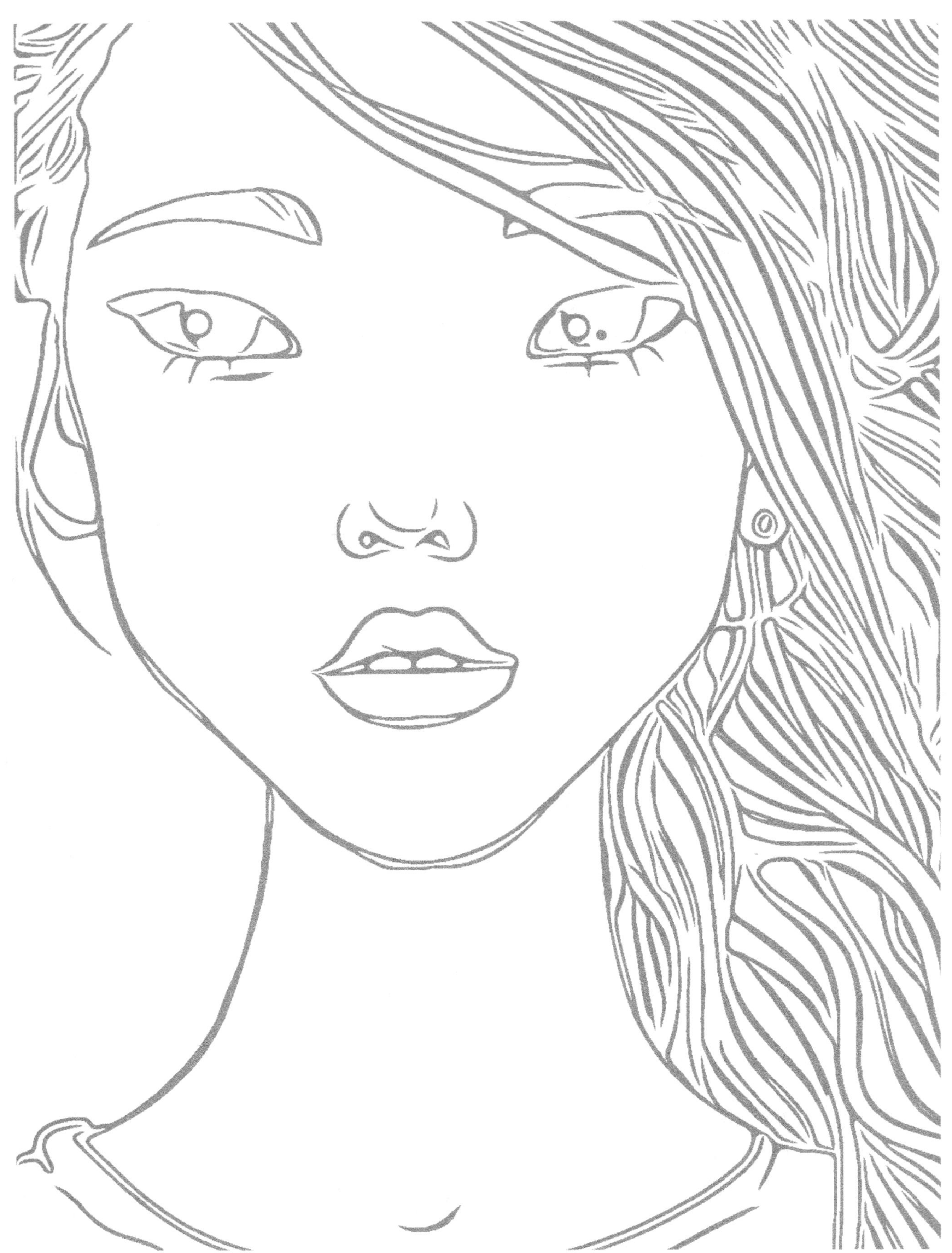

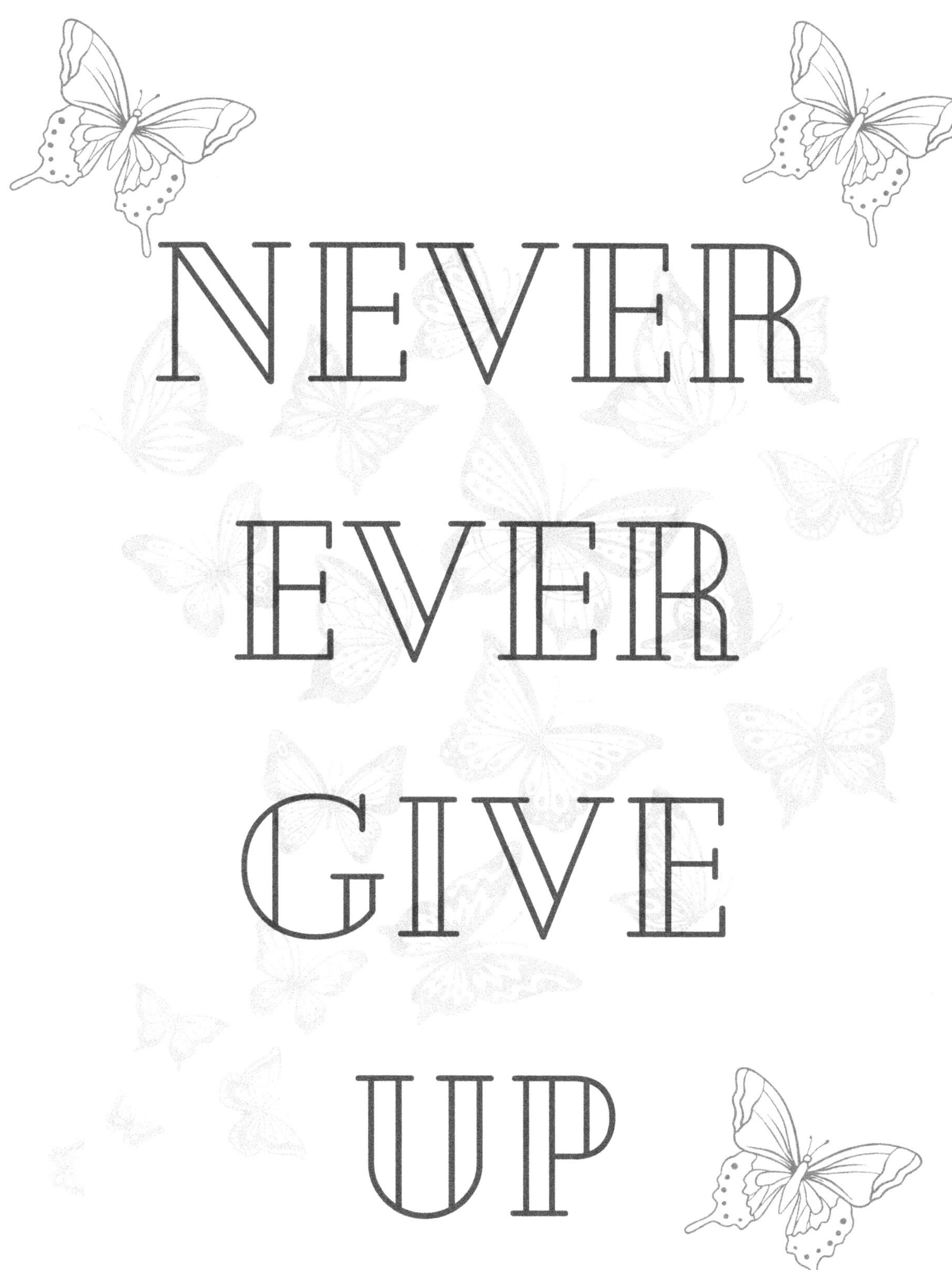
NEVER
EVER
GIVE
UP

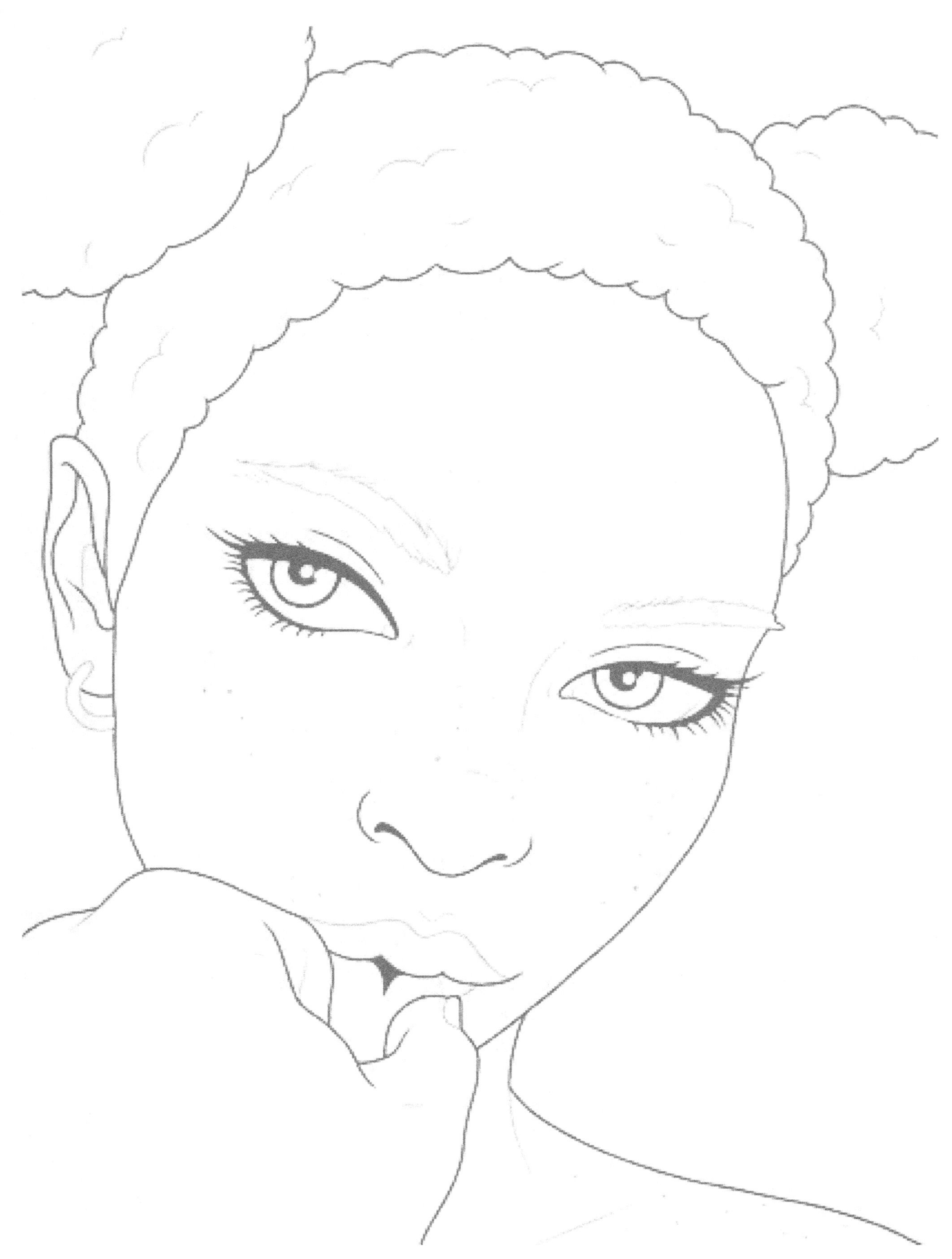

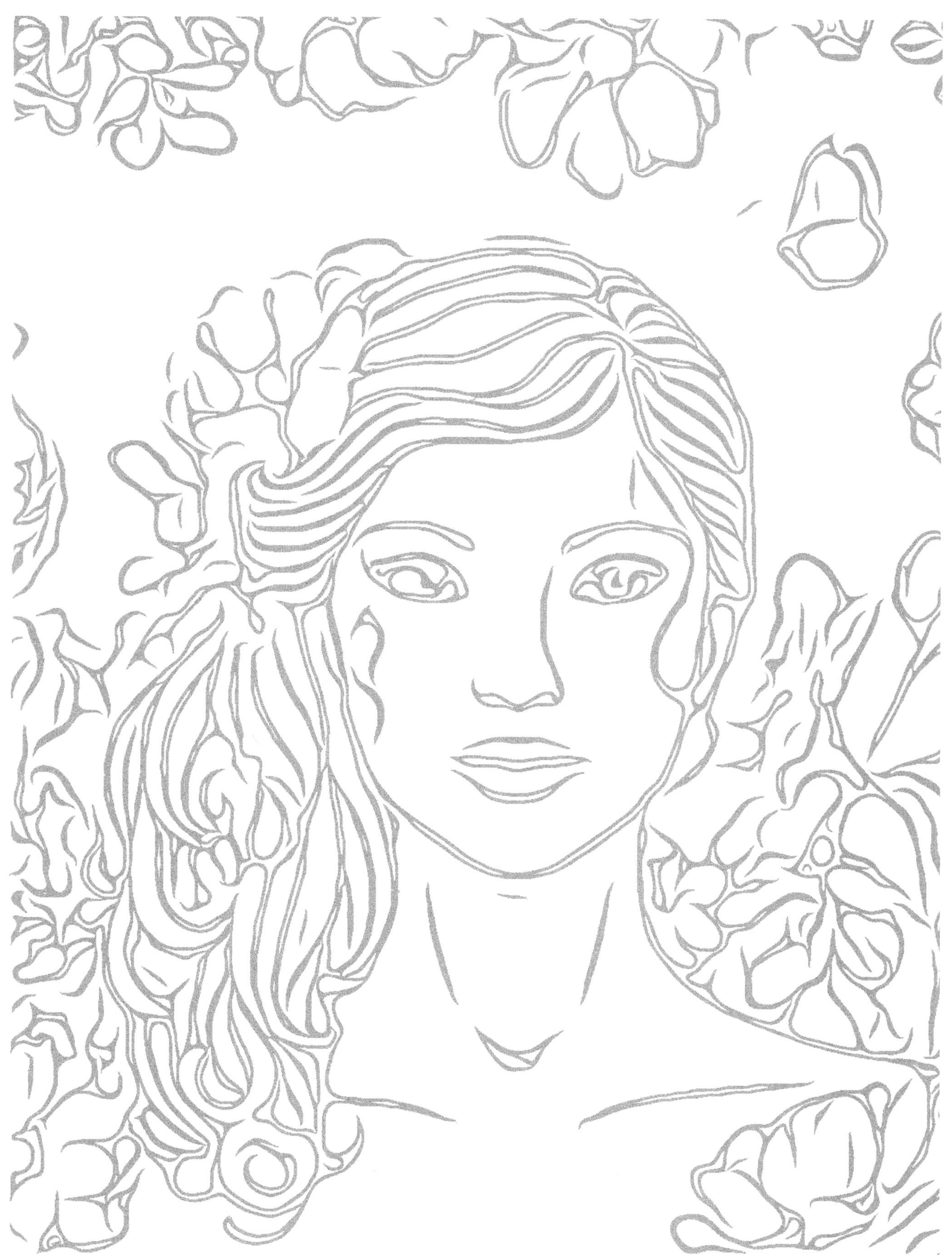

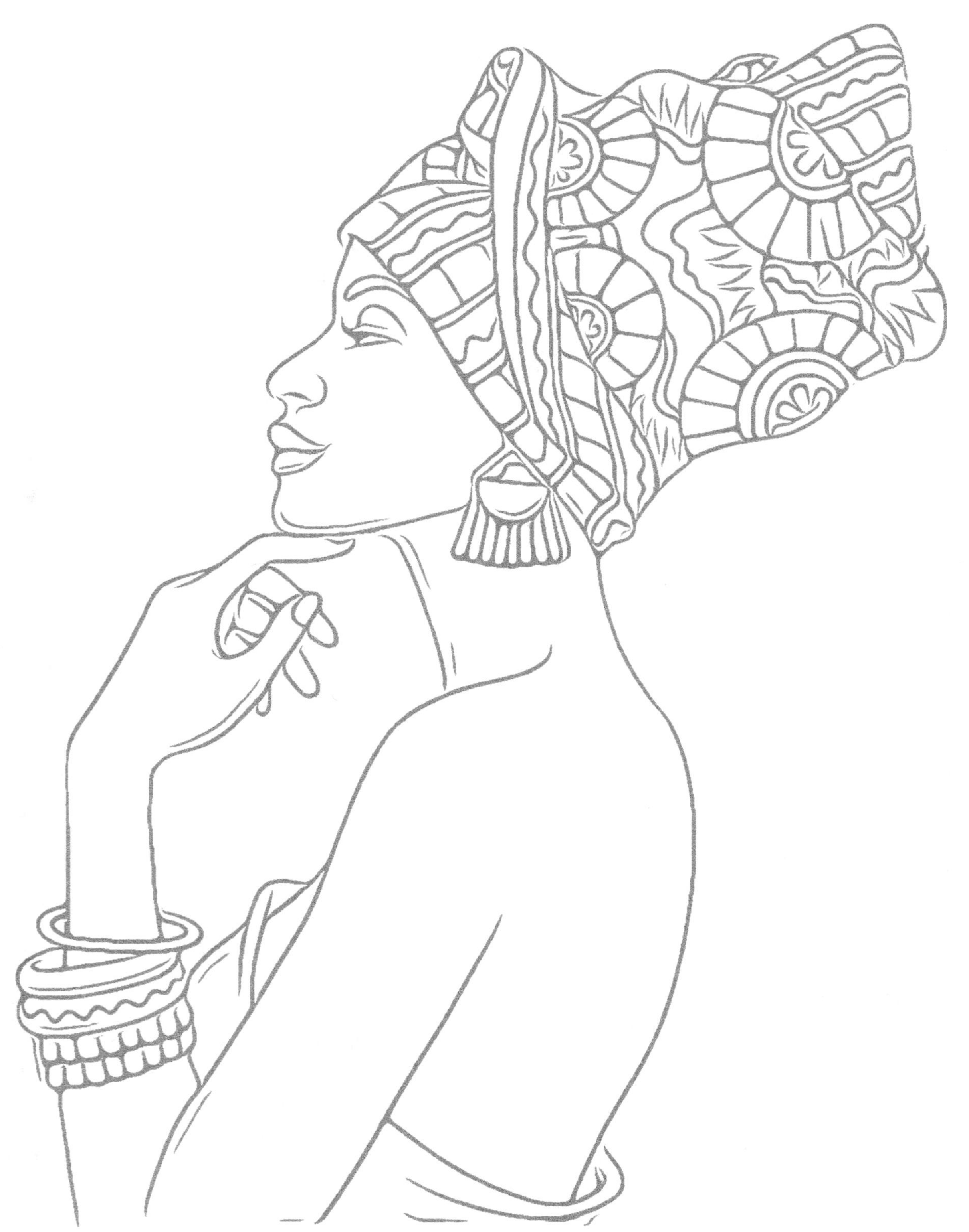

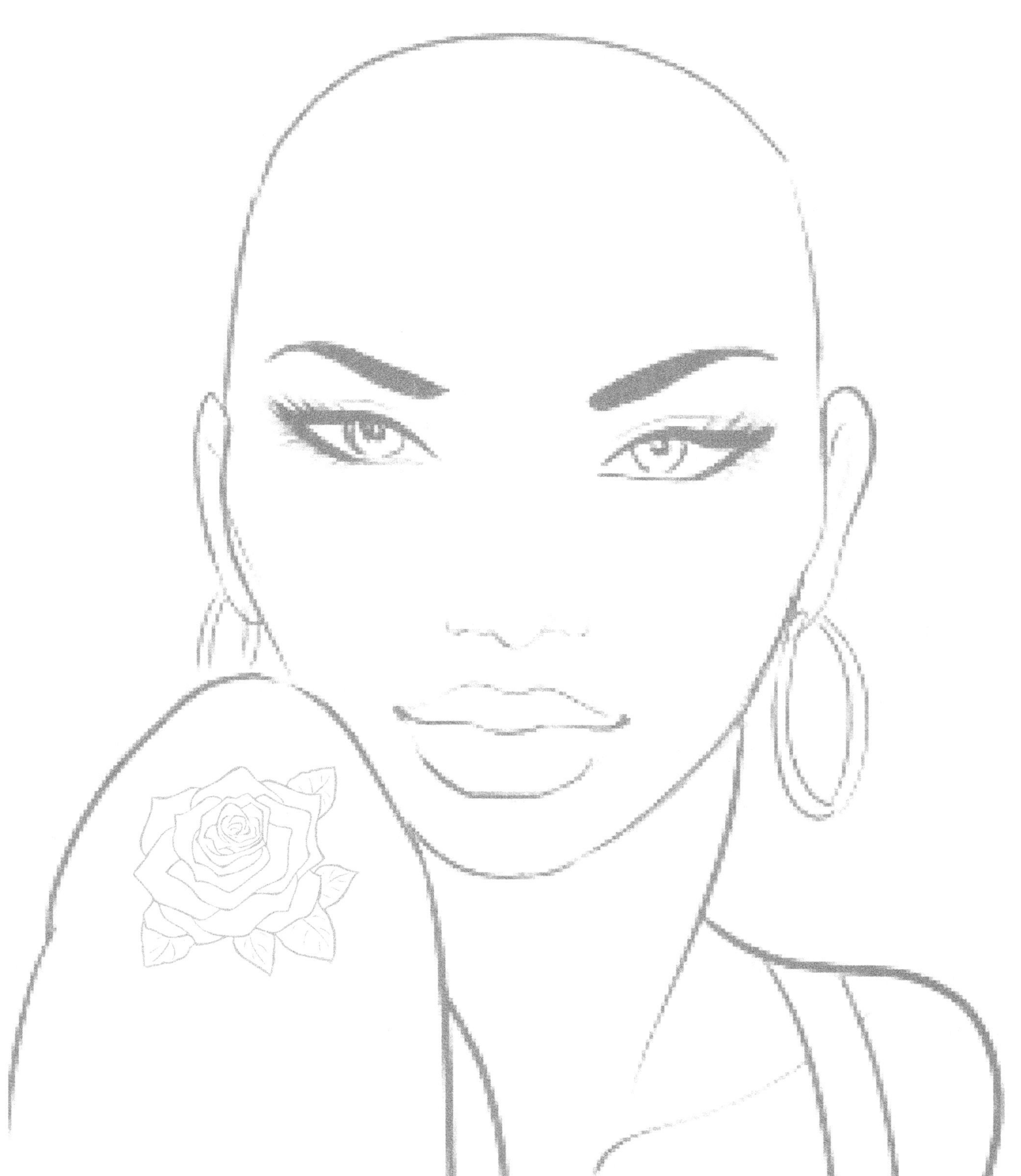

# YOU ARE BRAVE, YOU ARE STRONG, YOU ARE SMART!

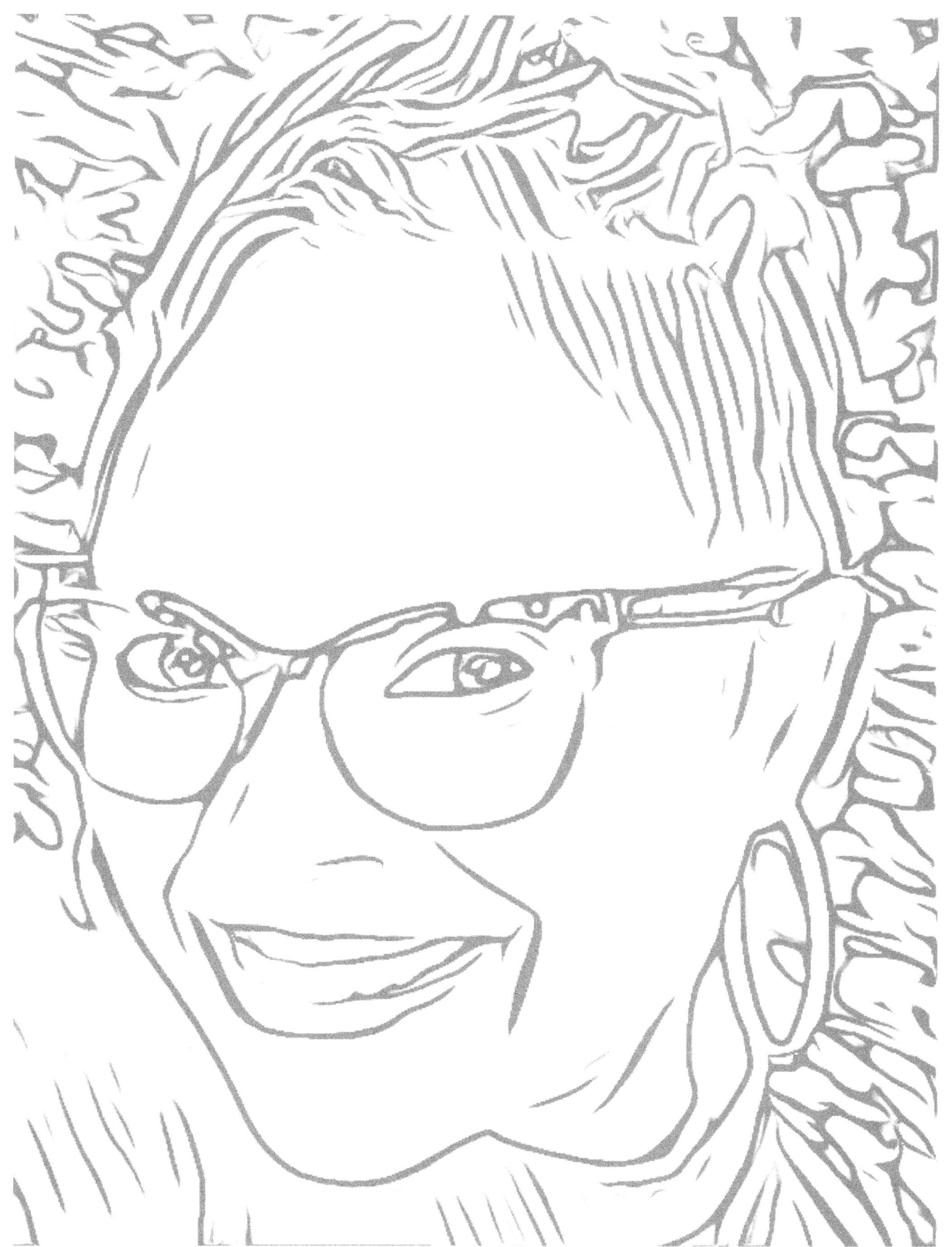

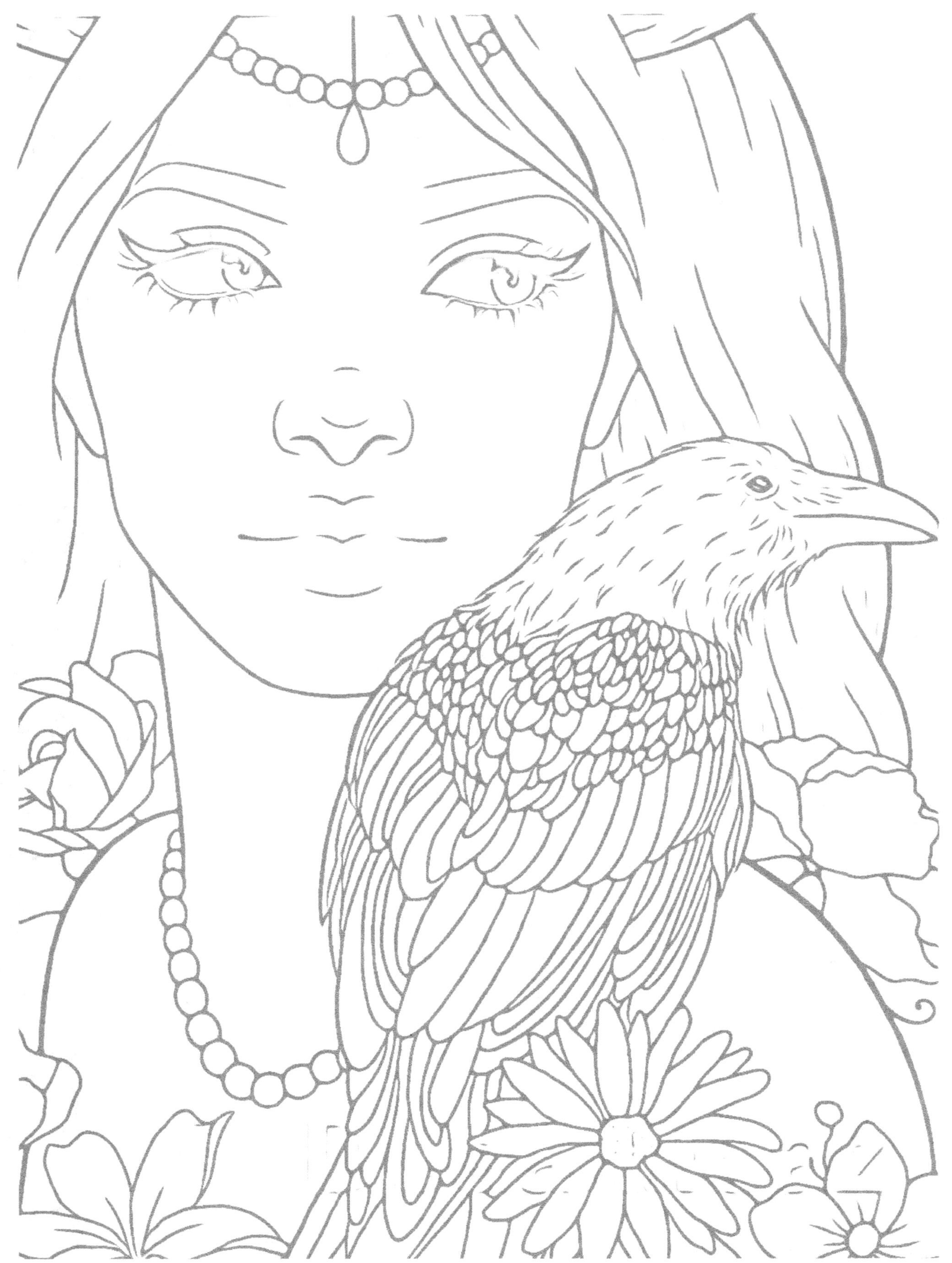

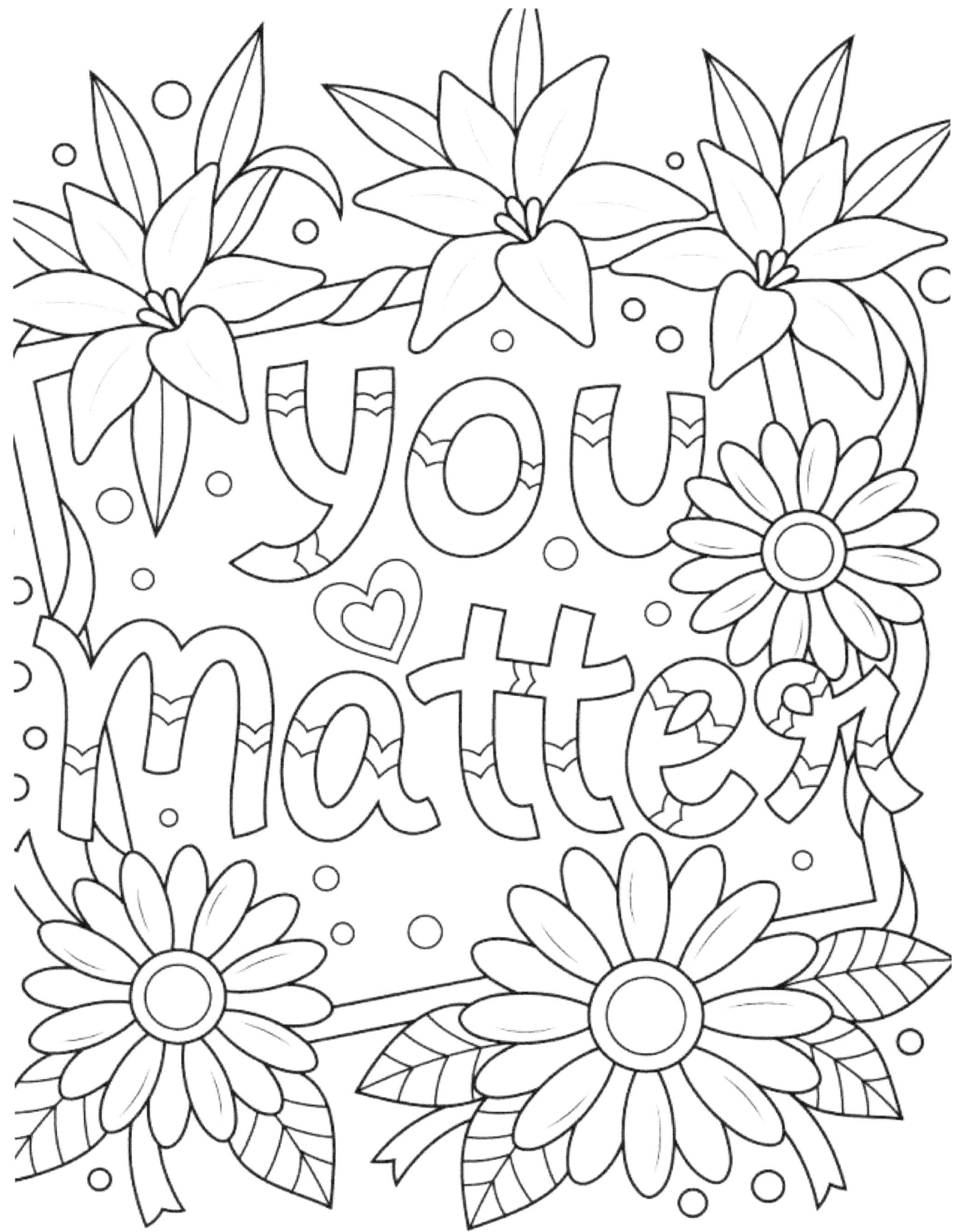

you matter

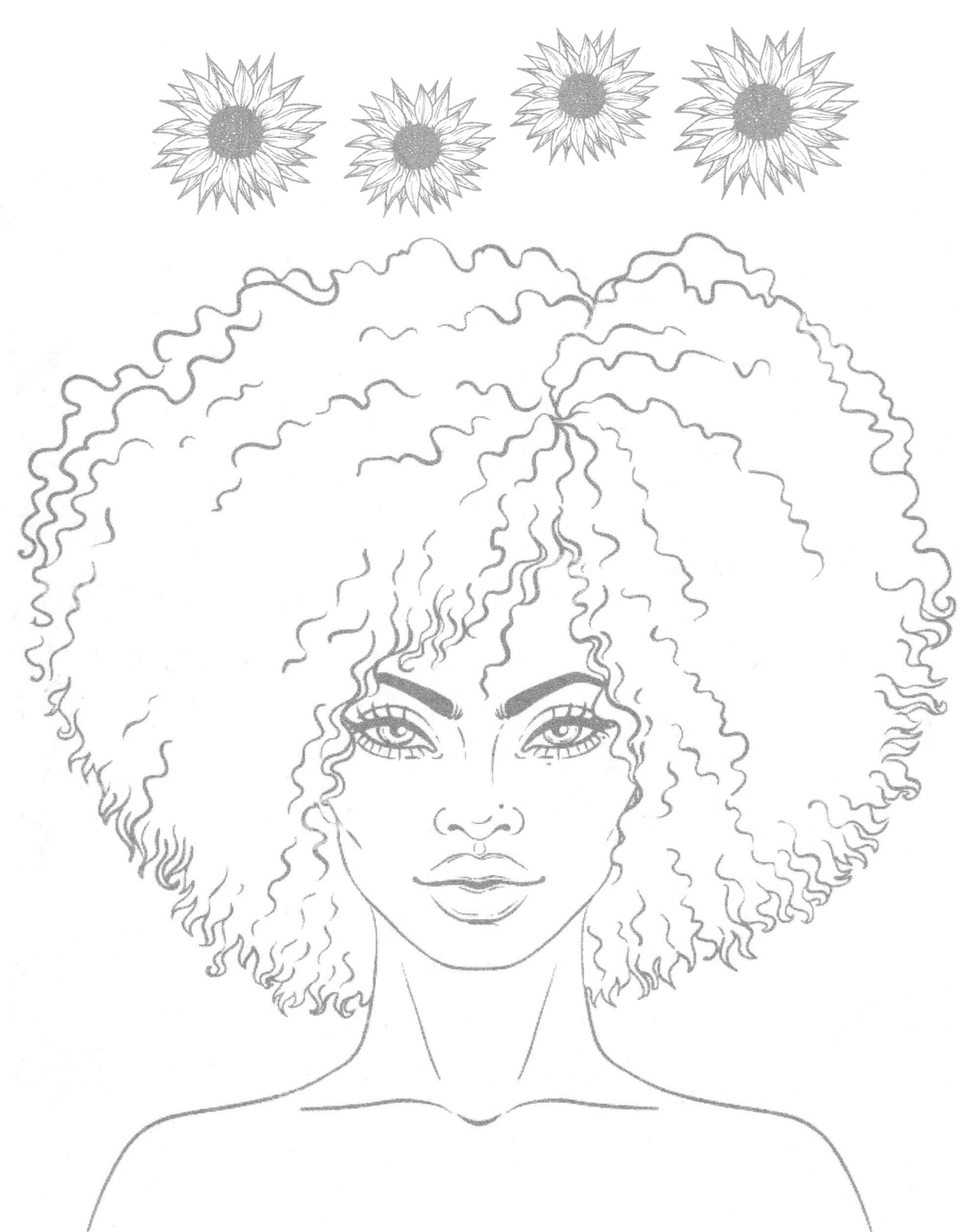

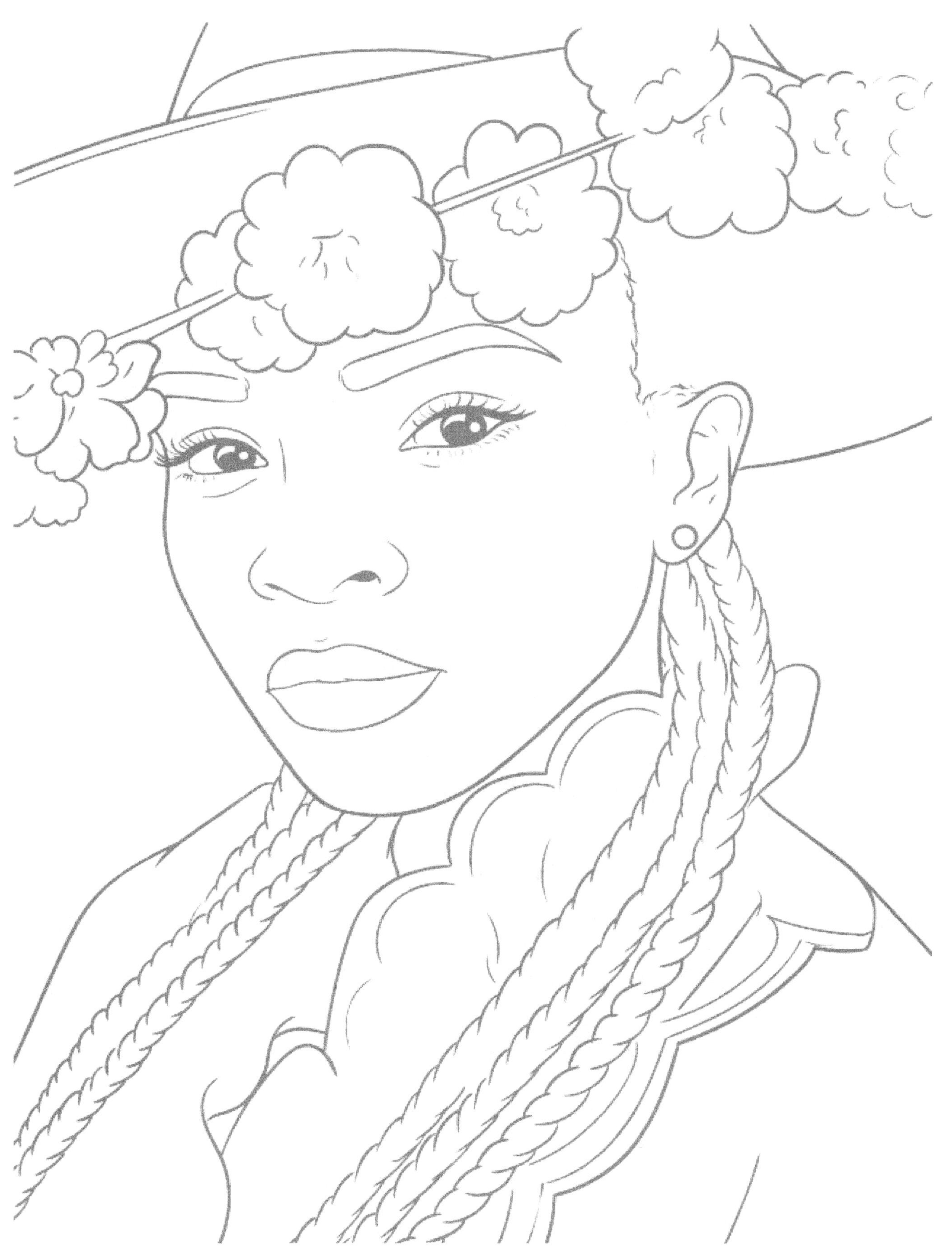

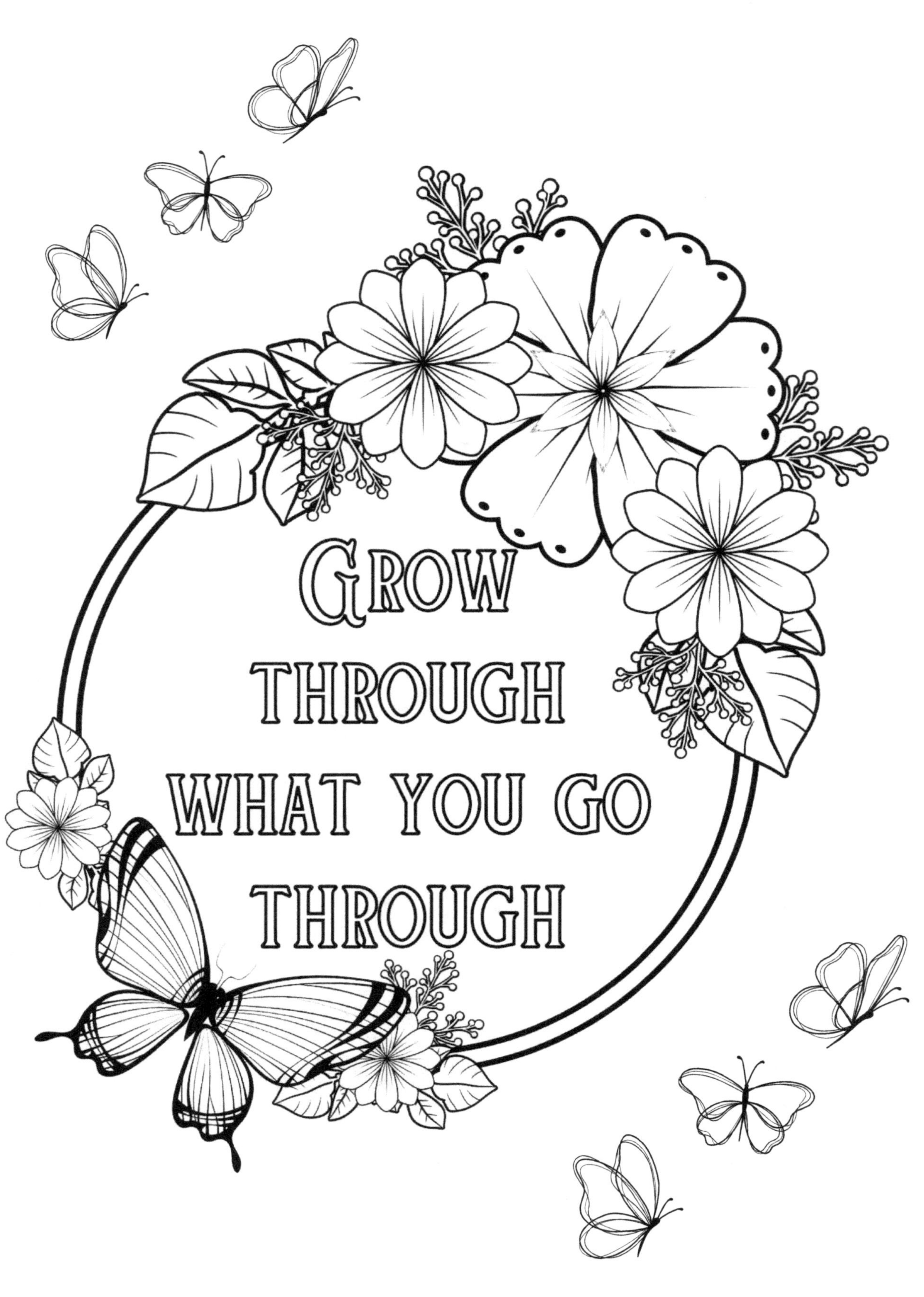

Grow
through
what you go
through

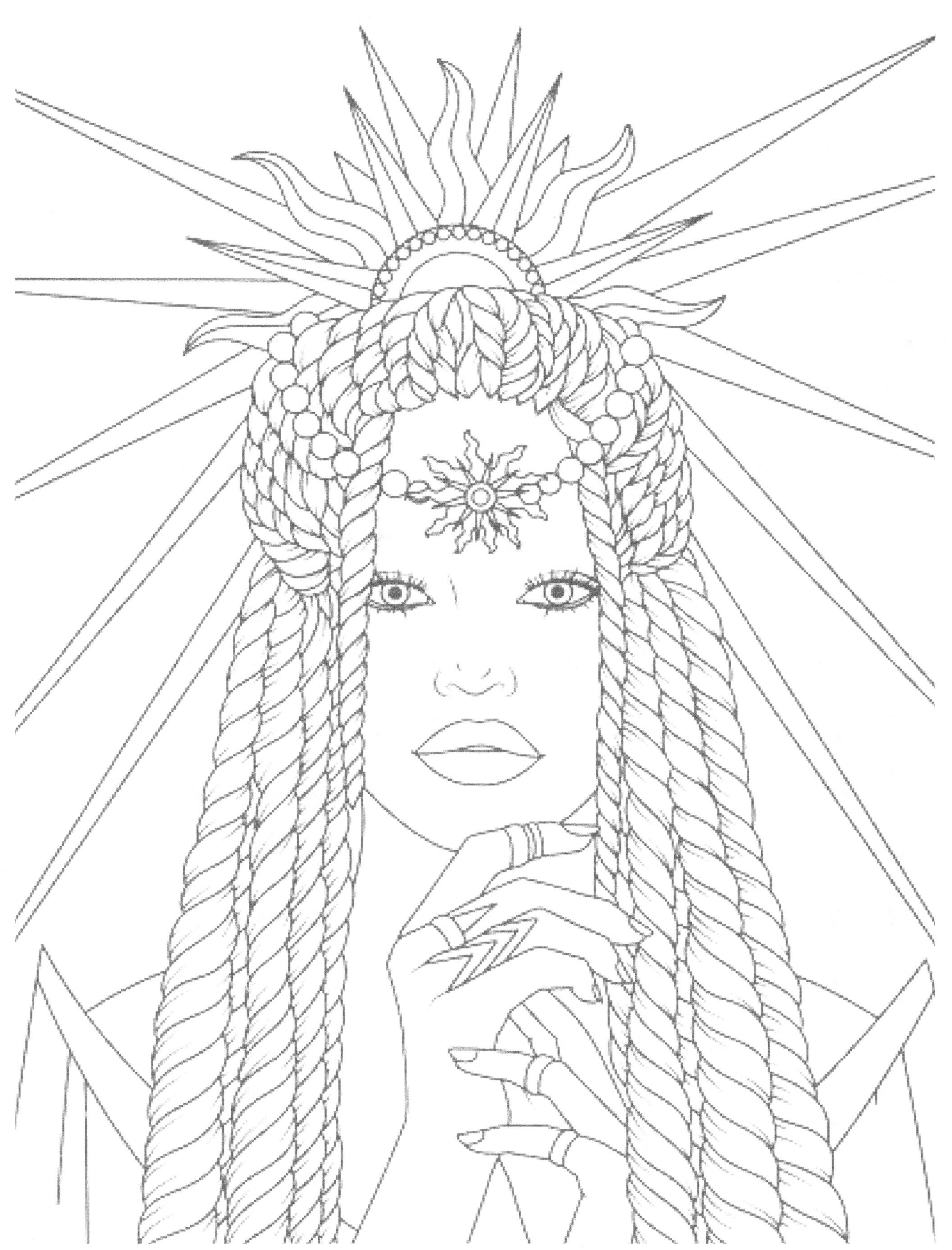

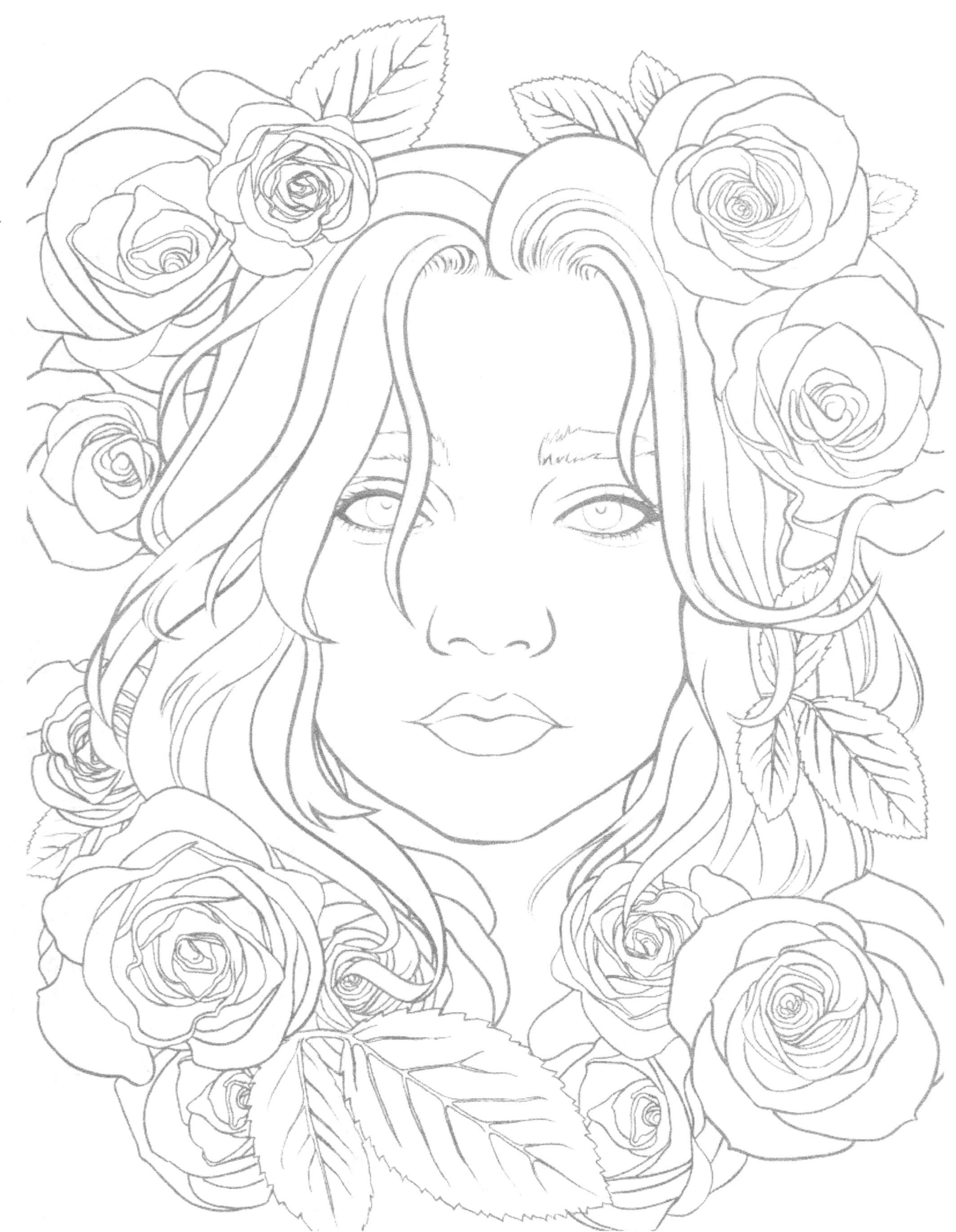

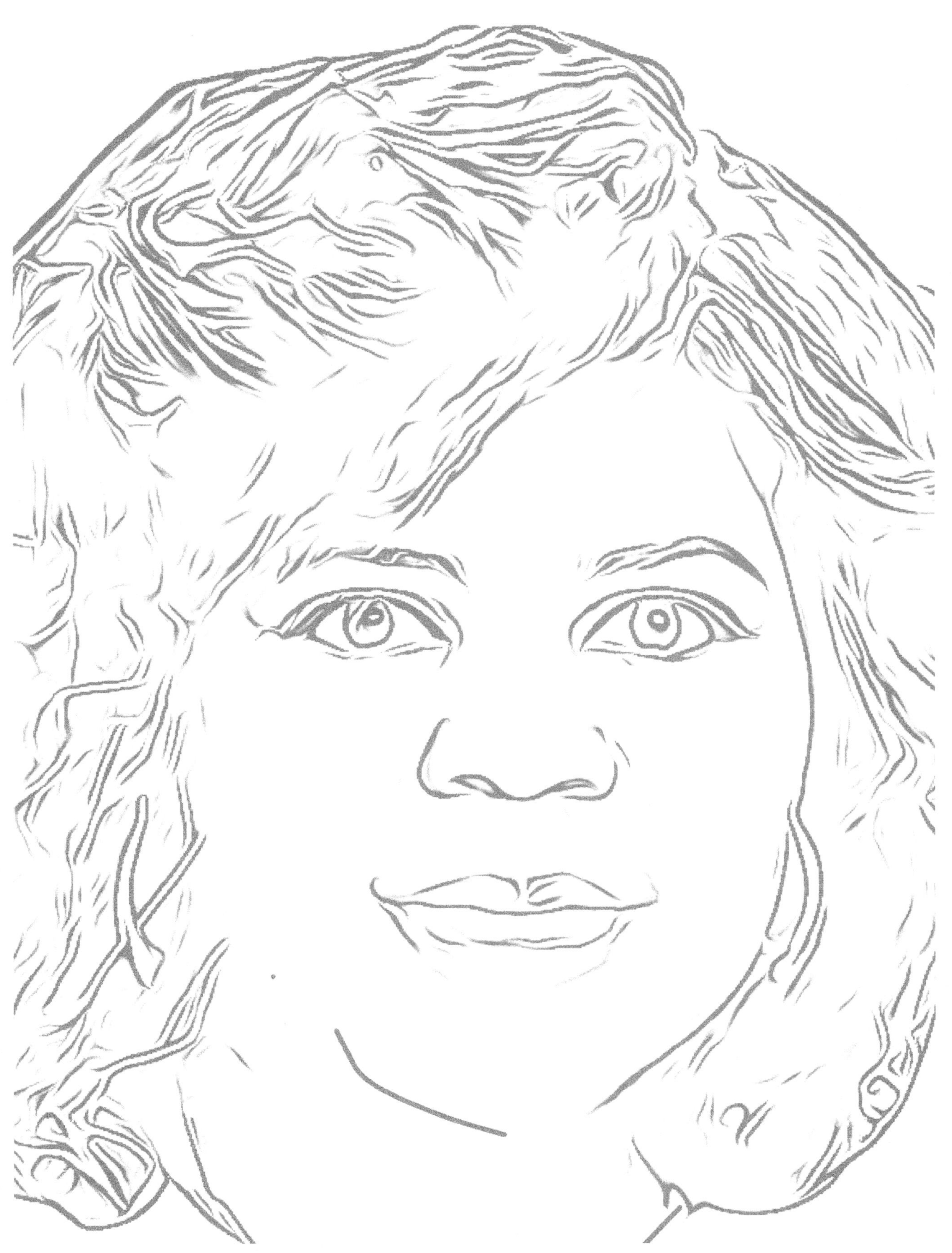

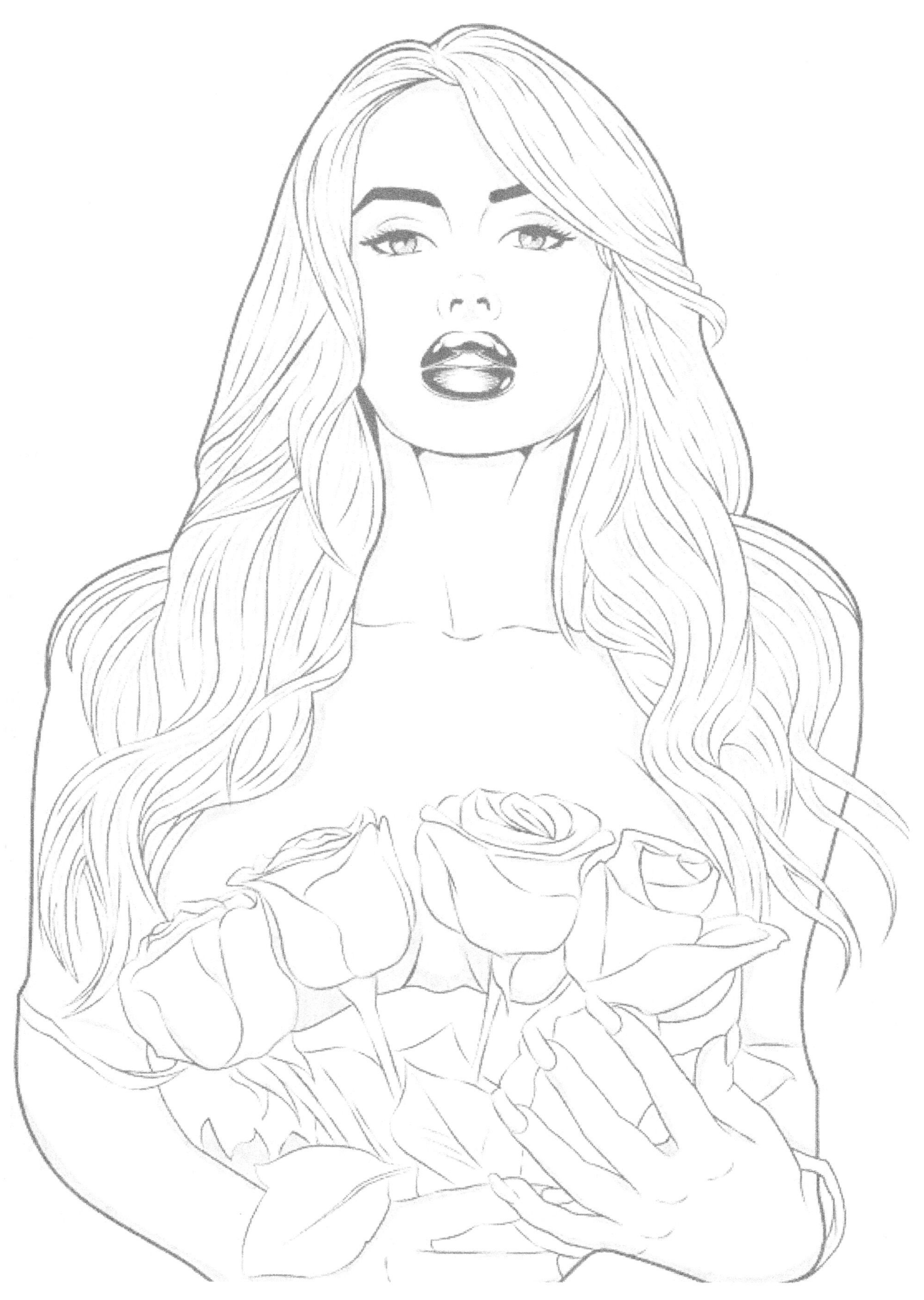

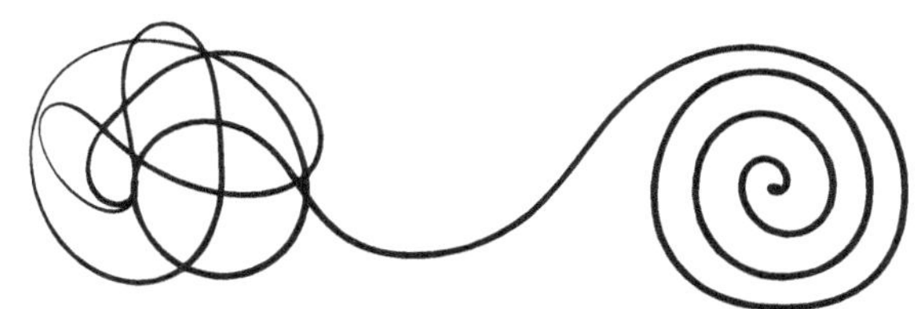

# I CREATE HAPPINESS BY APPRECIATING THE LITTLE THINGS IN LIFE.

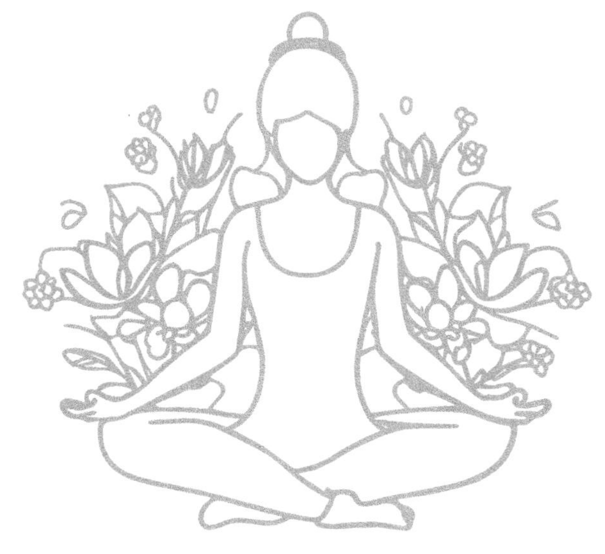

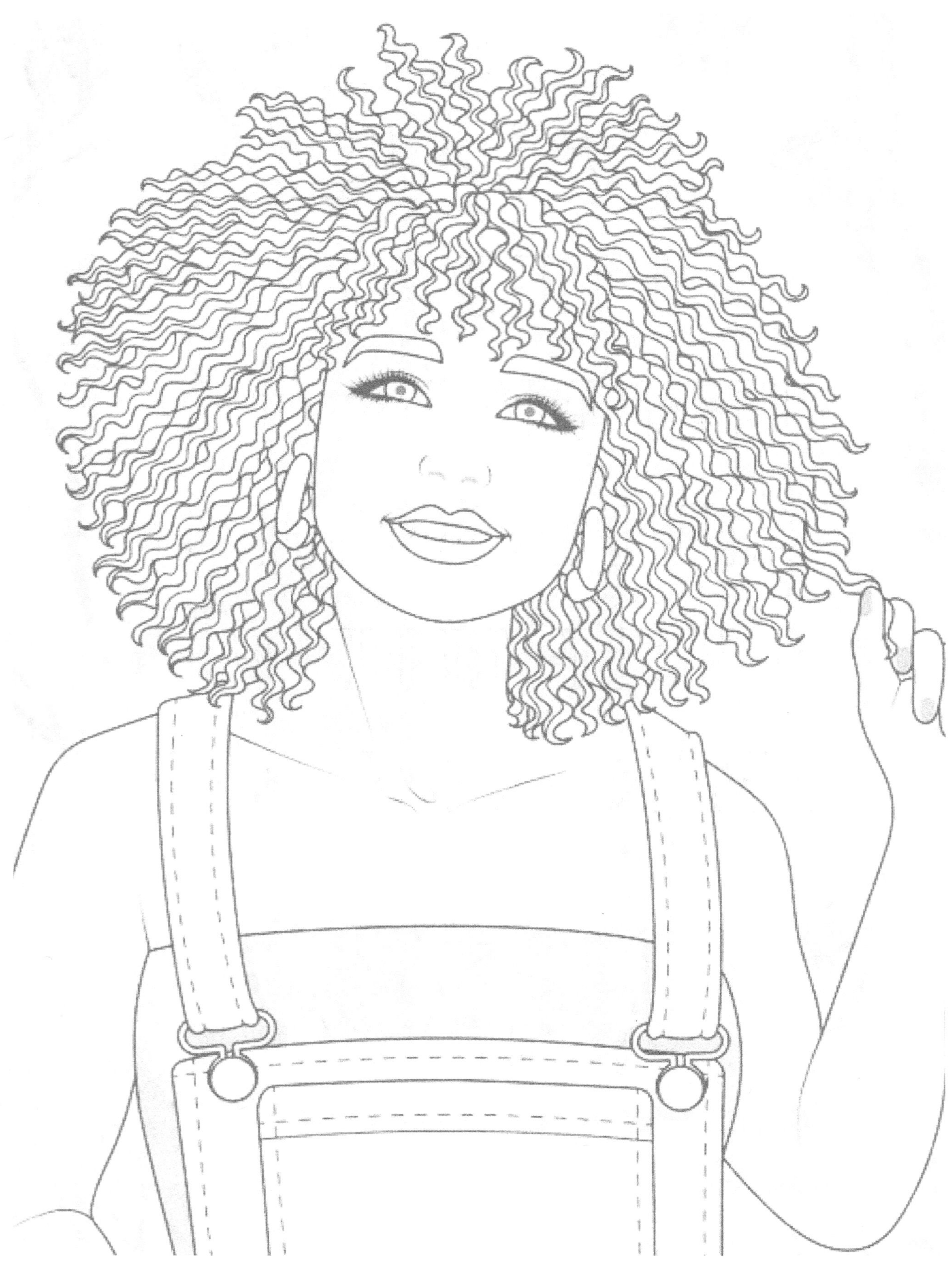

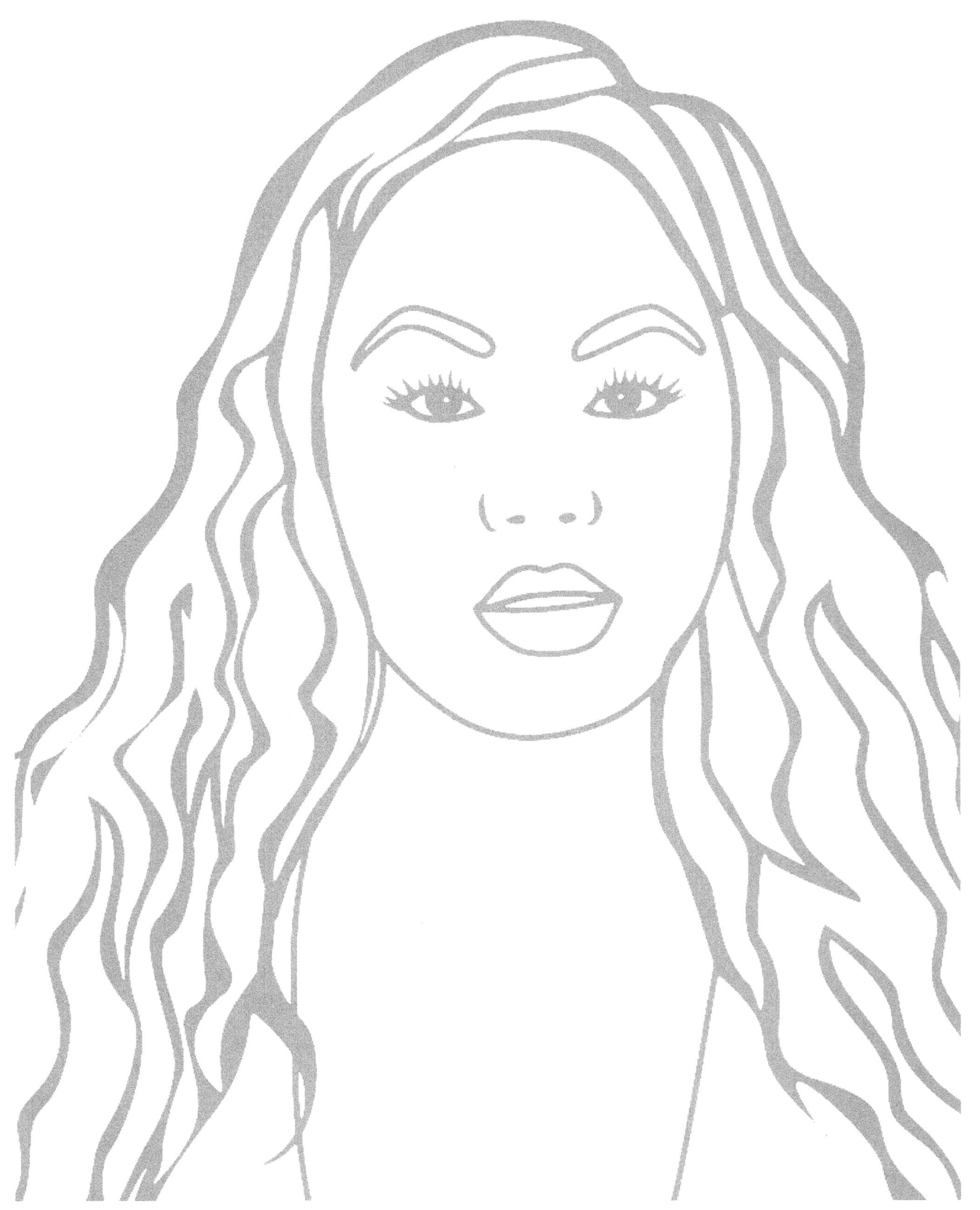

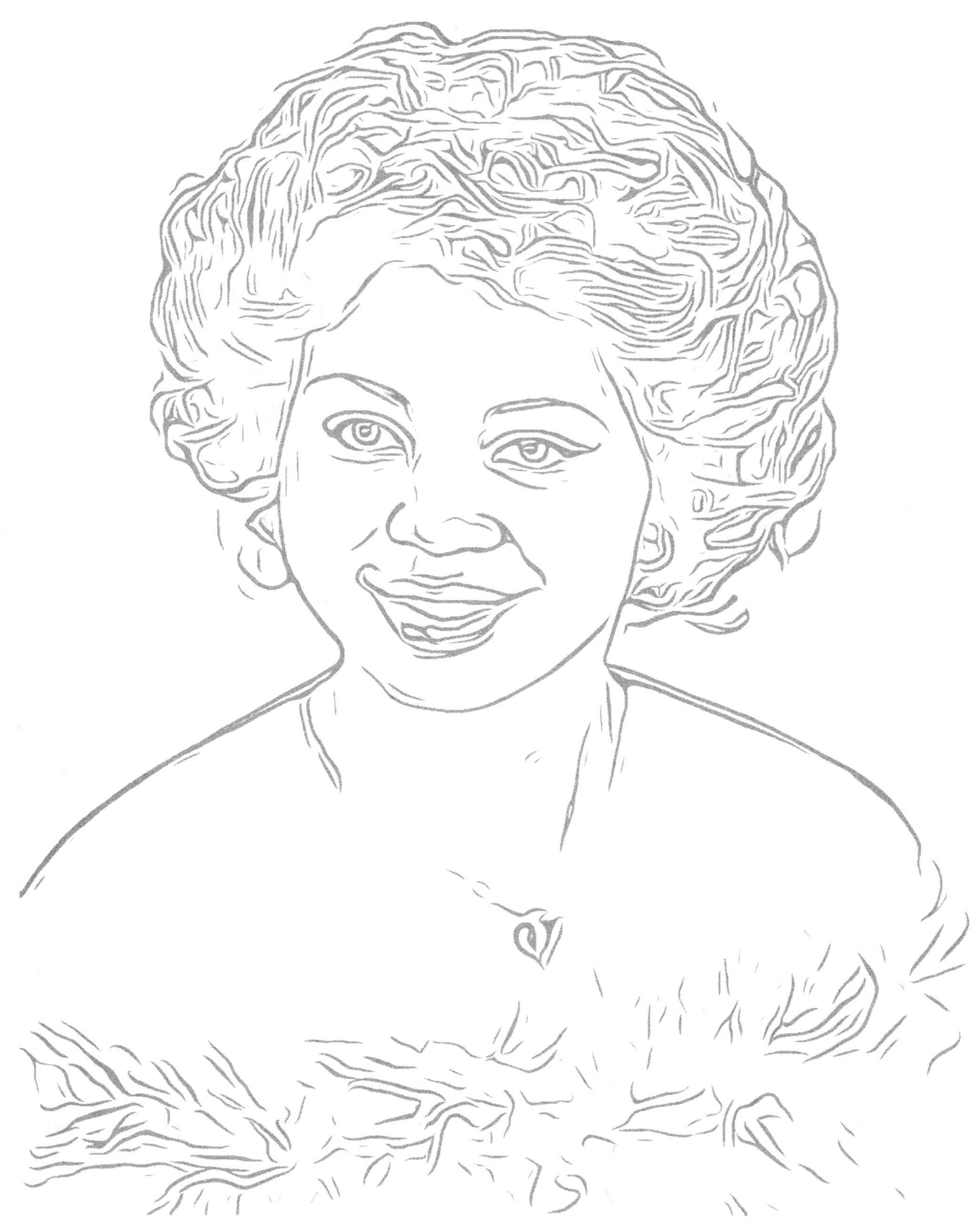

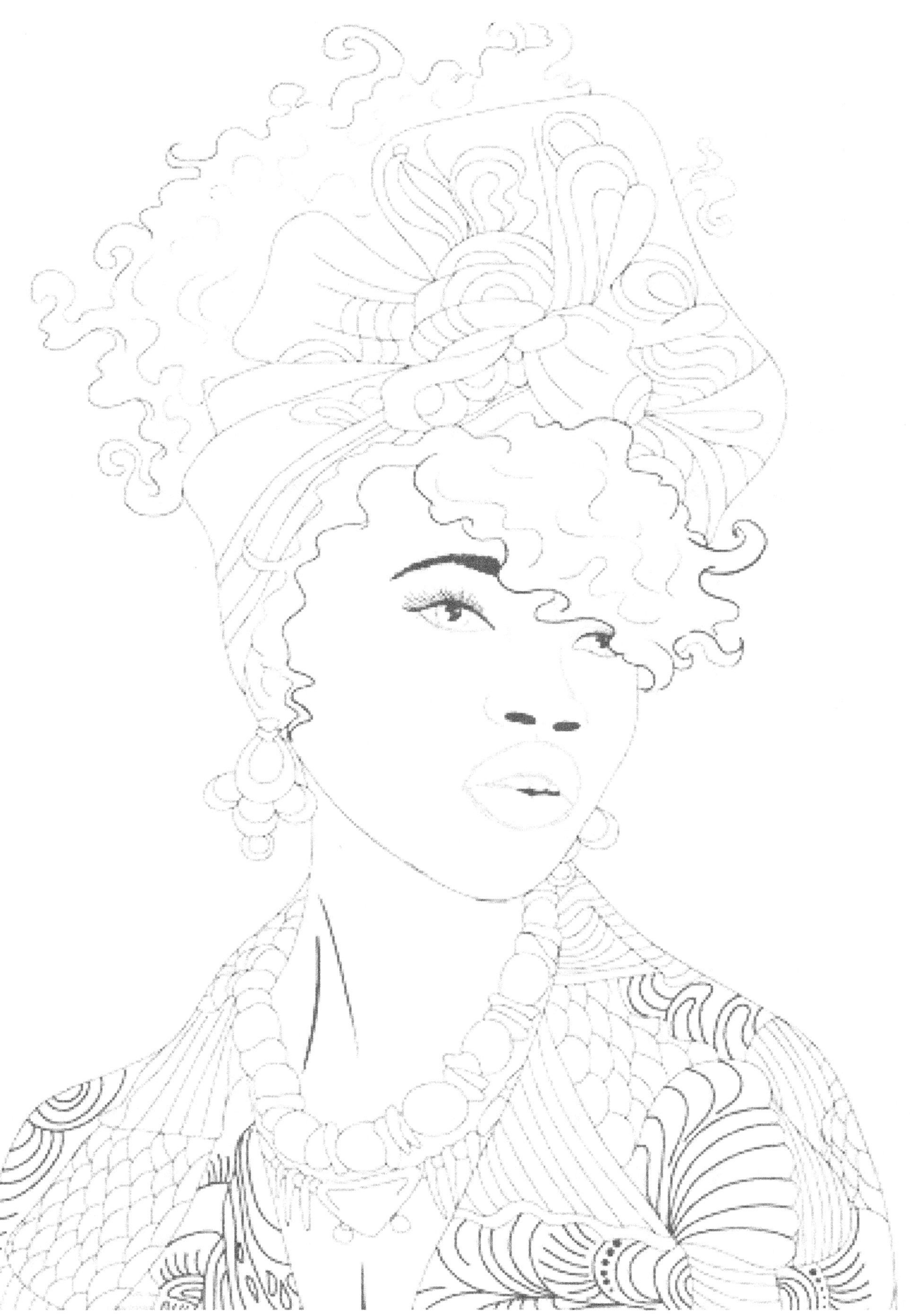

I AM
COMFORTABLE
IN MY OWN
SKIN.

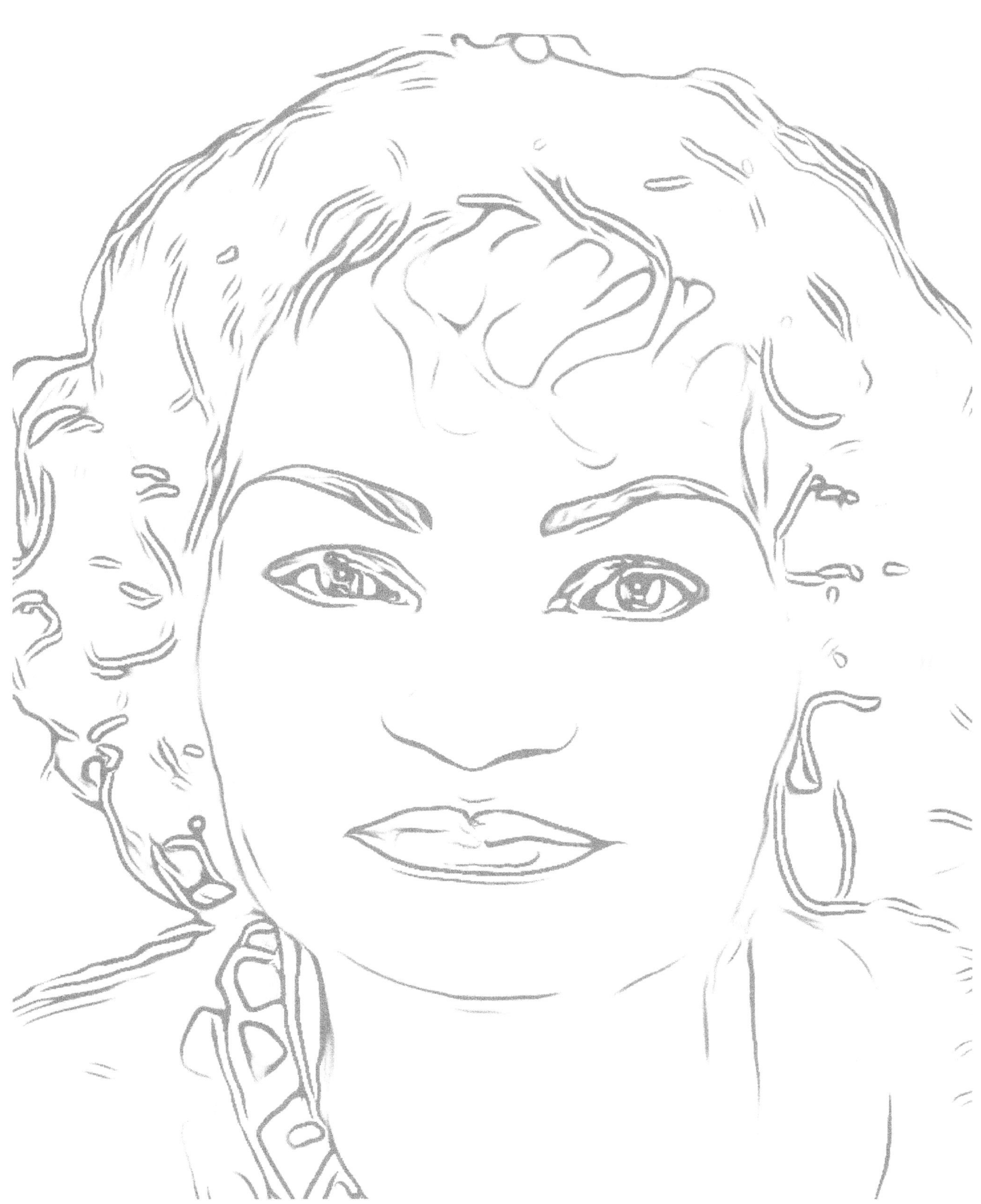

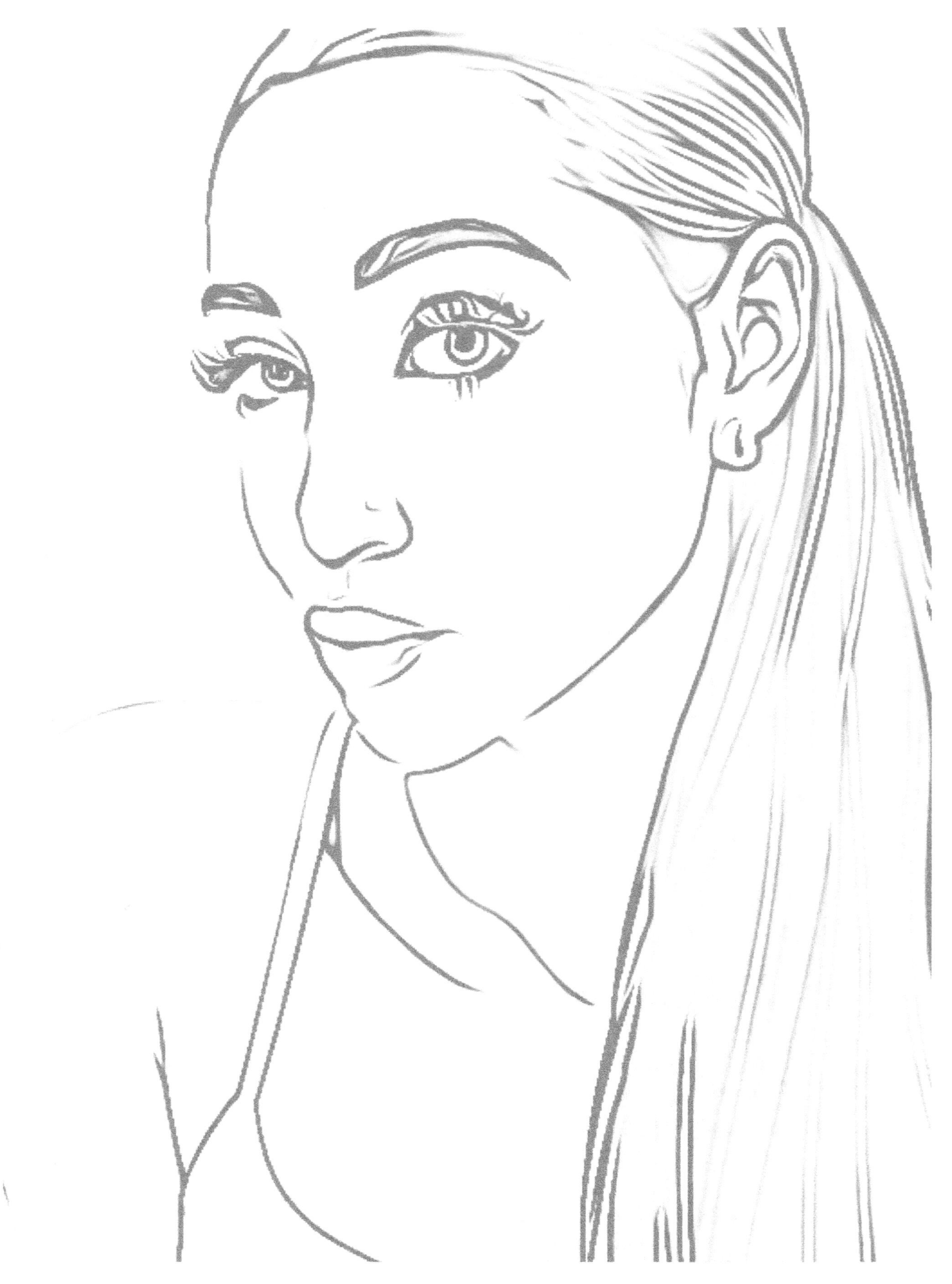

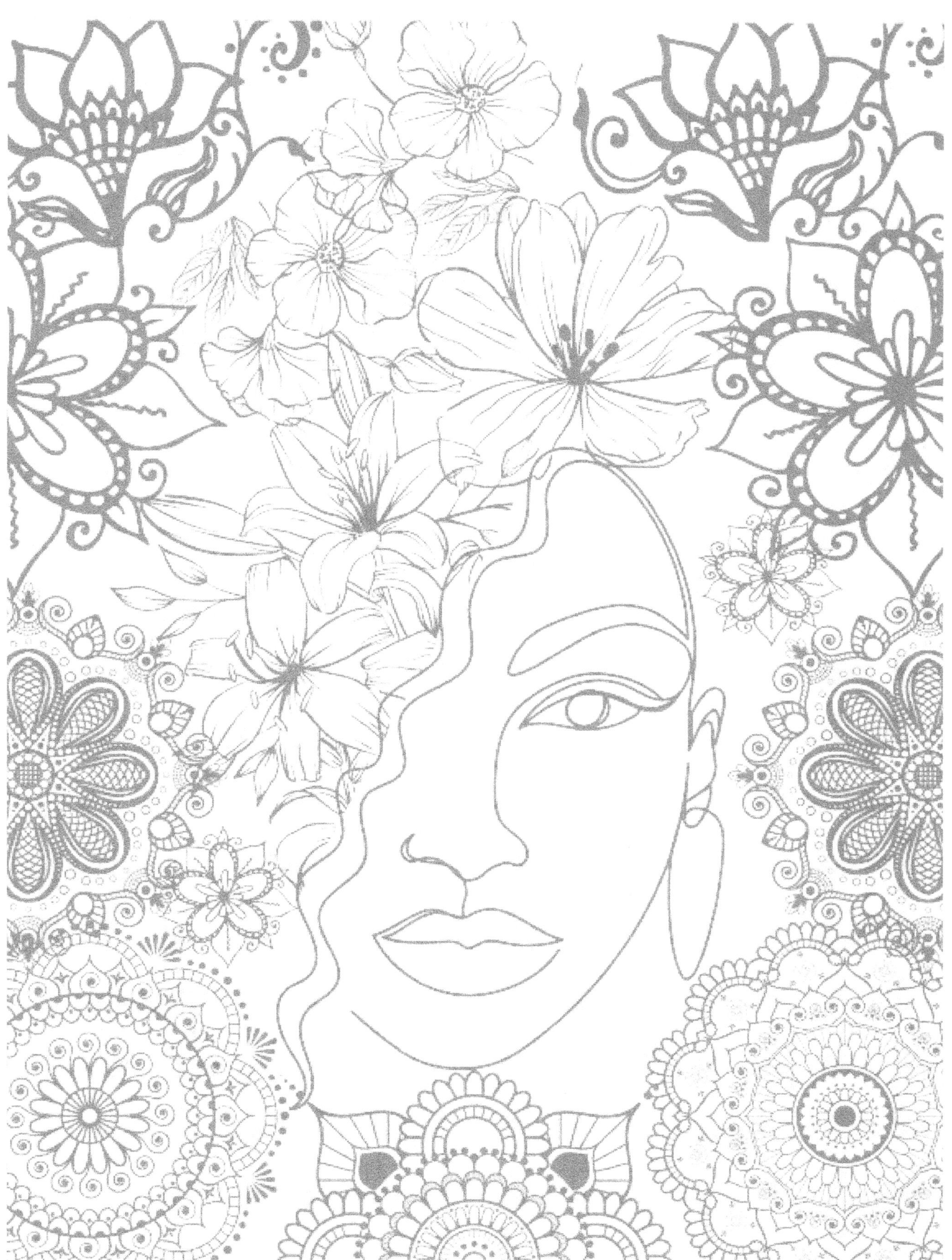

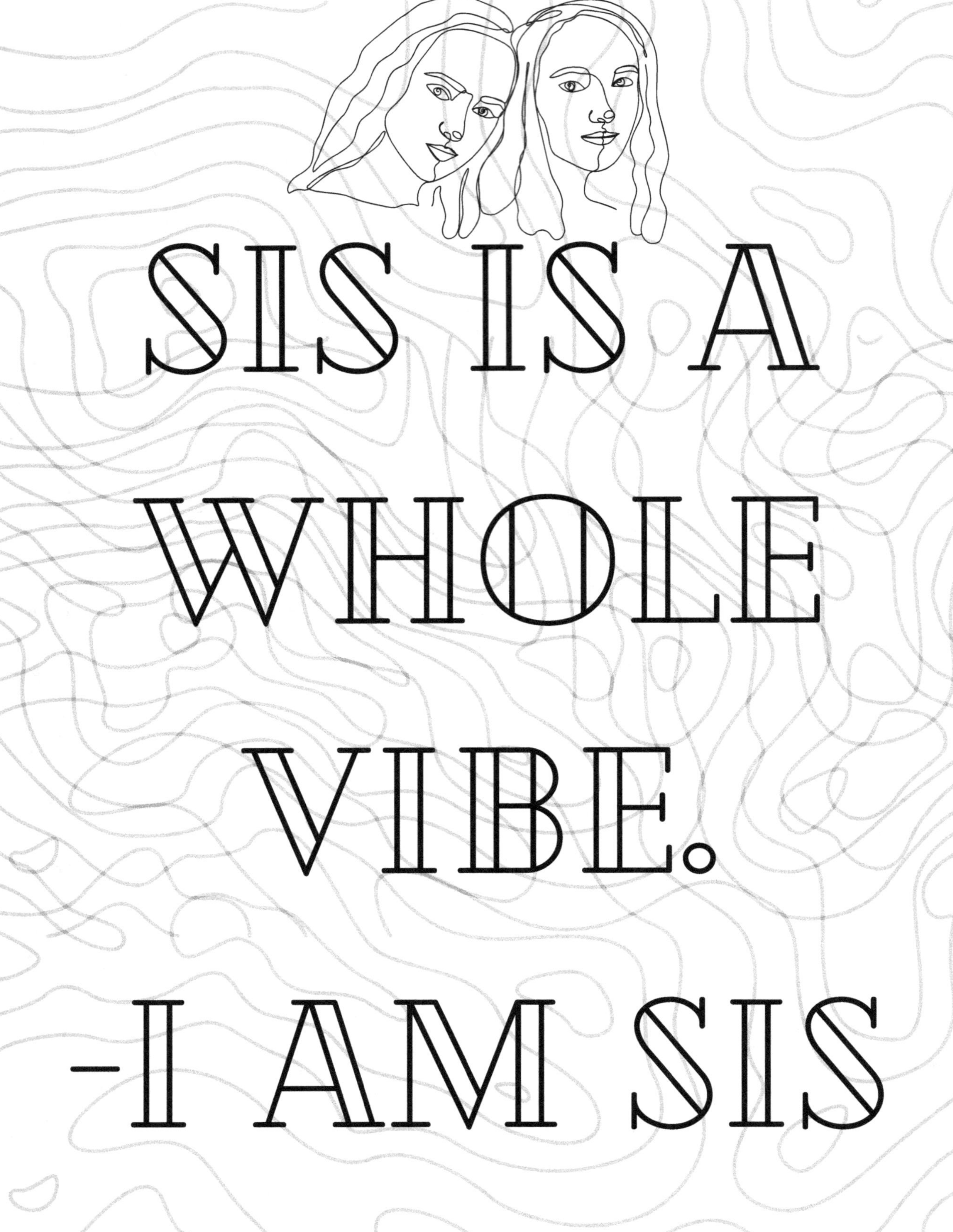

SIS IS A
WHOLE
VIBE.

-I AM SIS

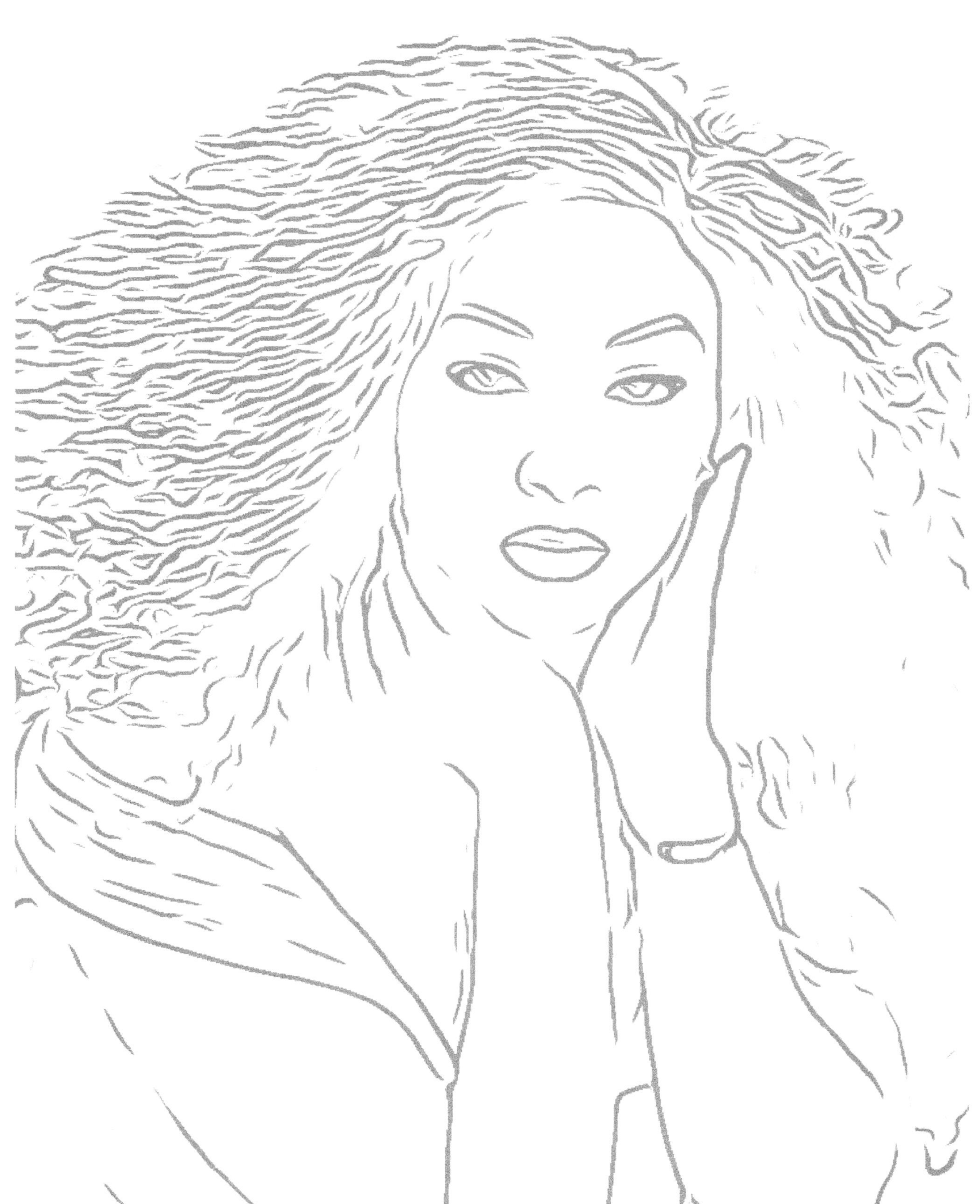

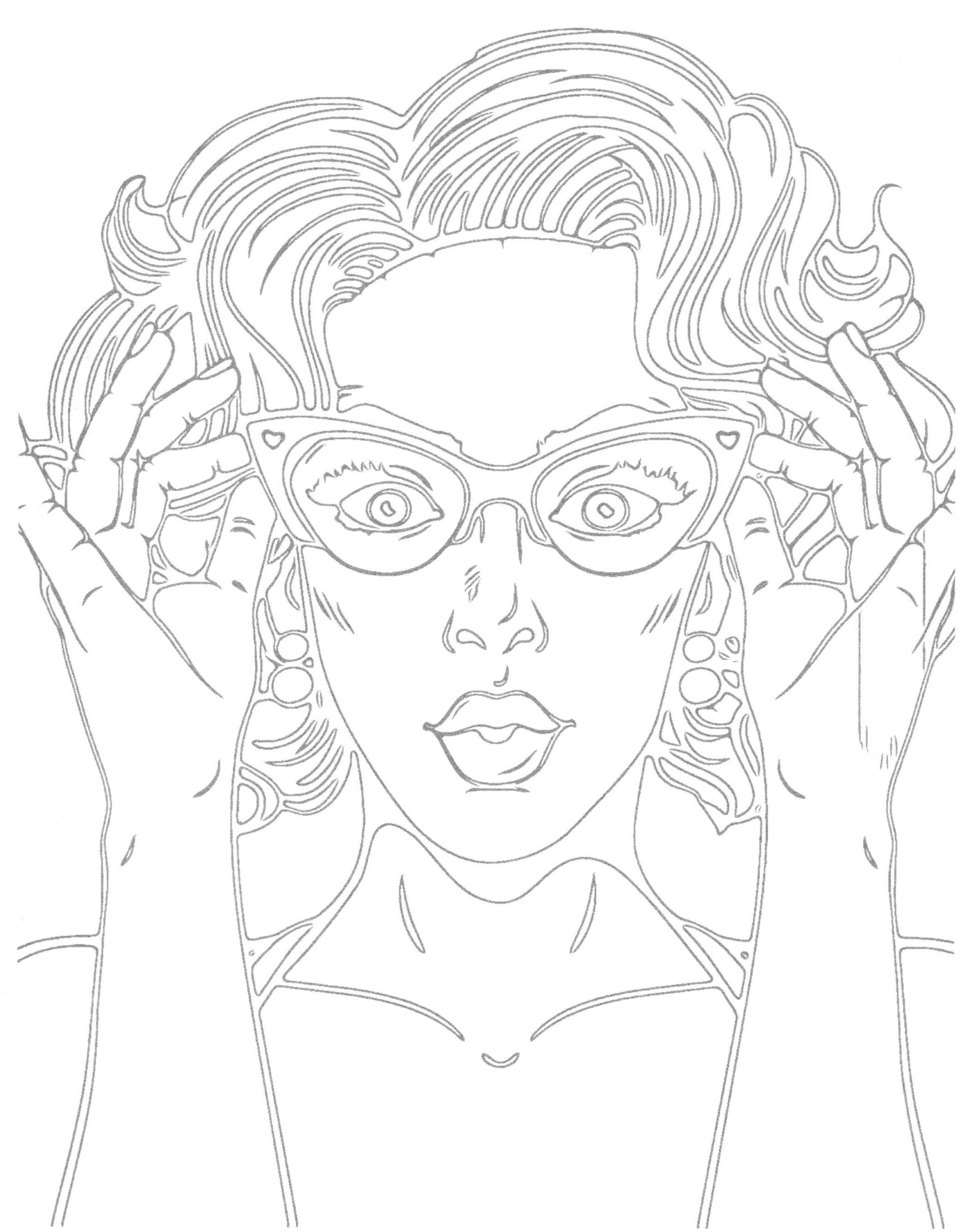

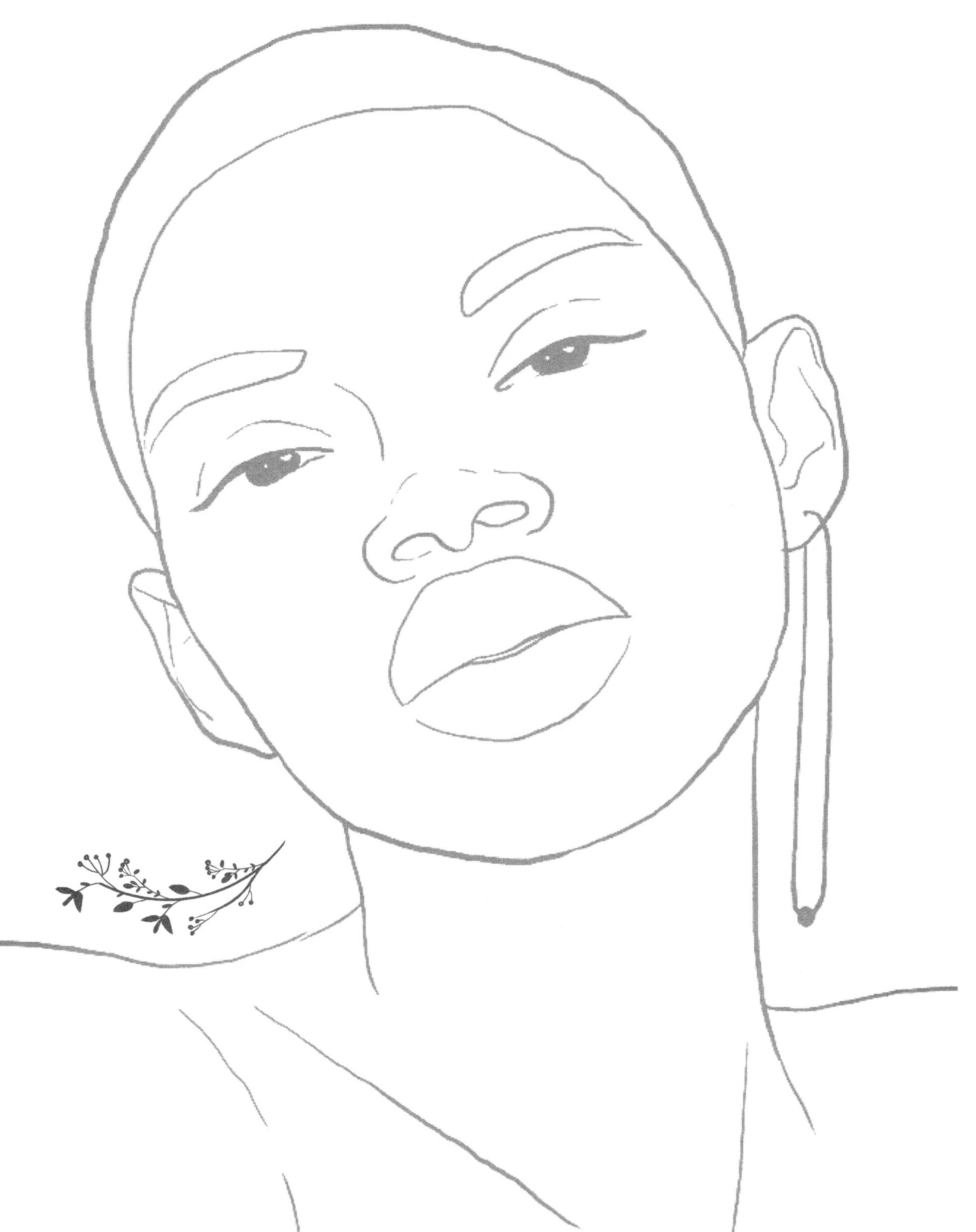

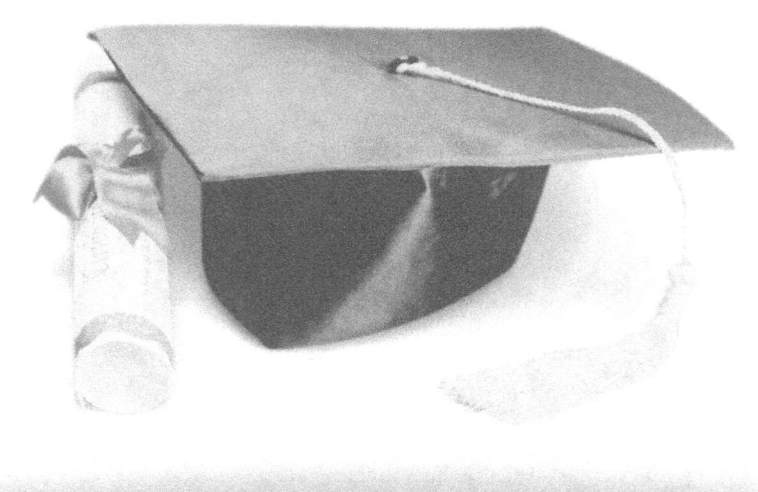

# SHE BELIEVED SHE COULD, SO SHE DID!

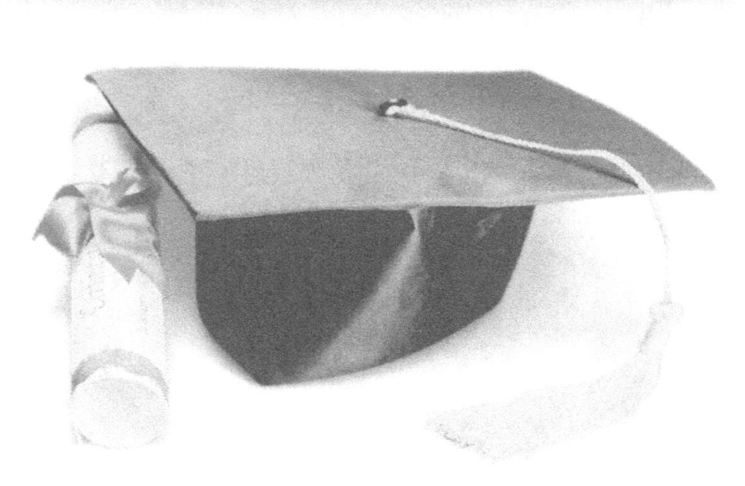

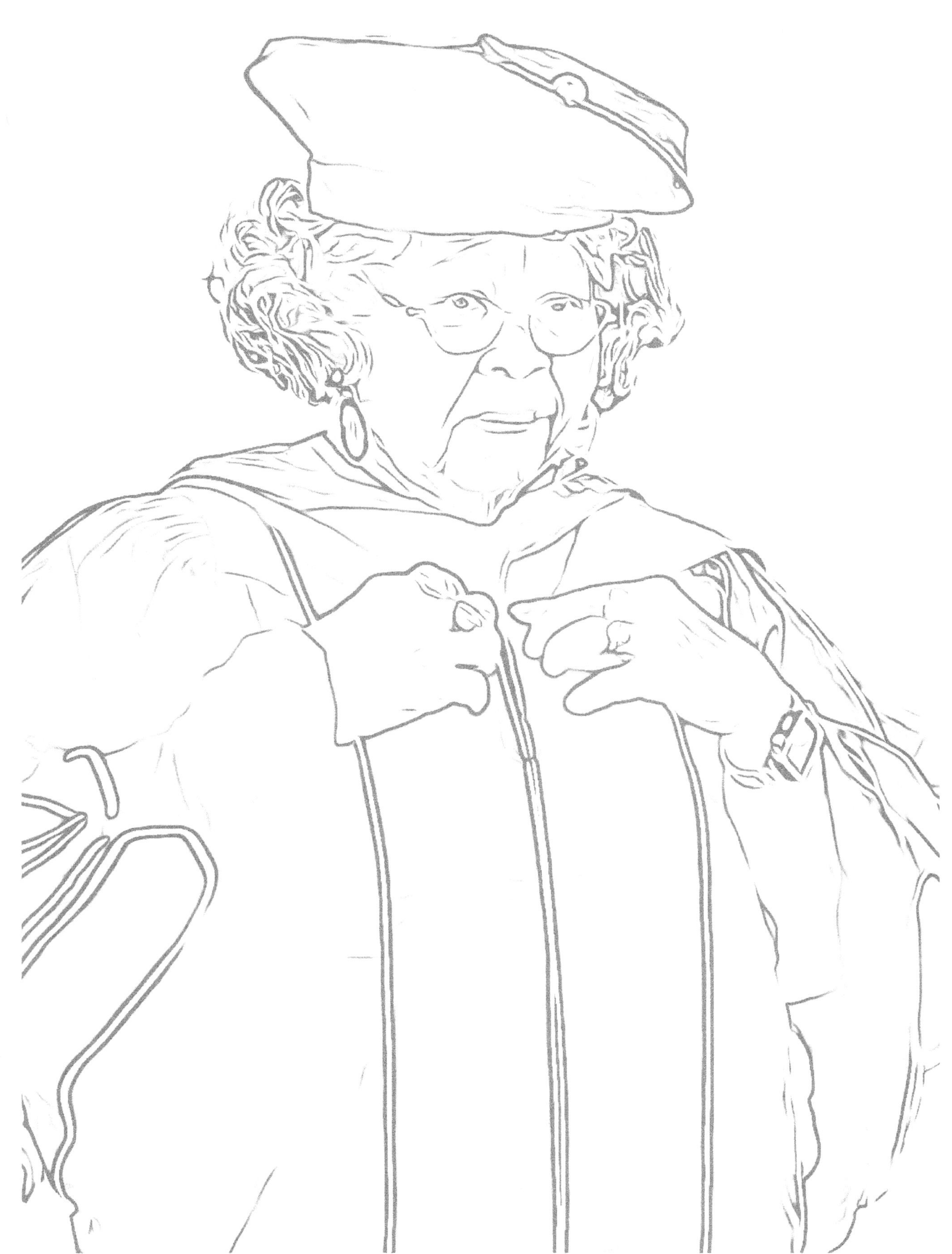

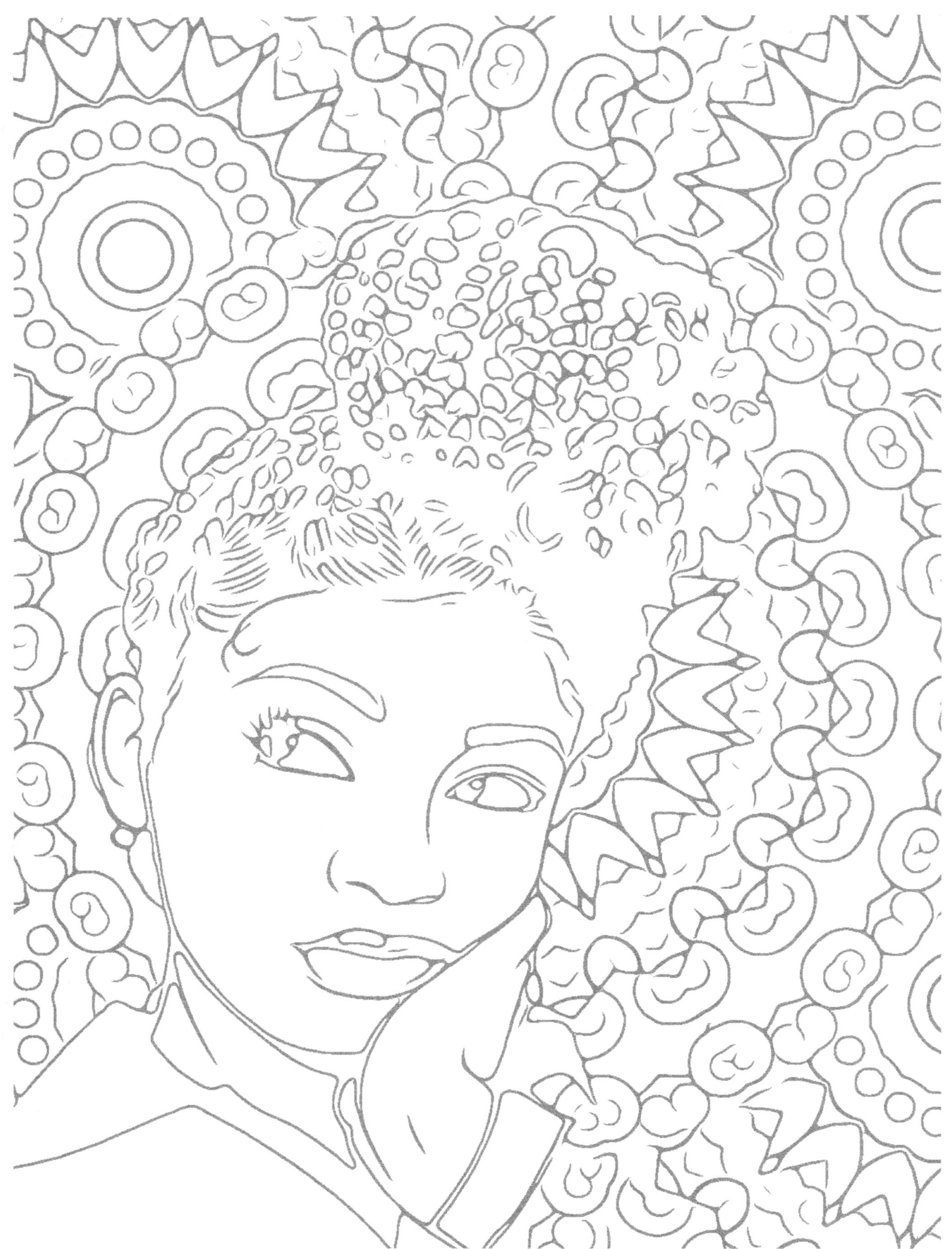

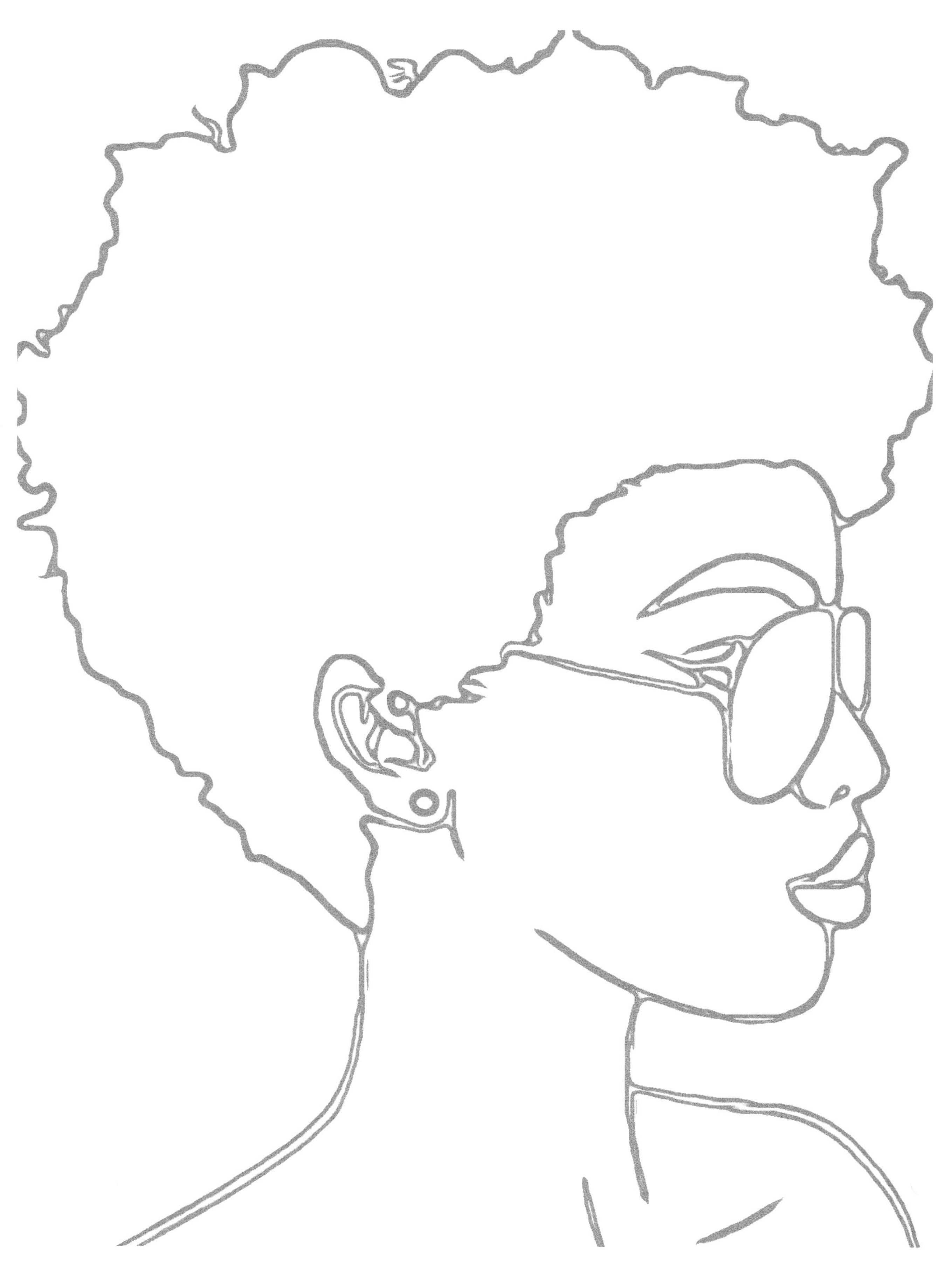

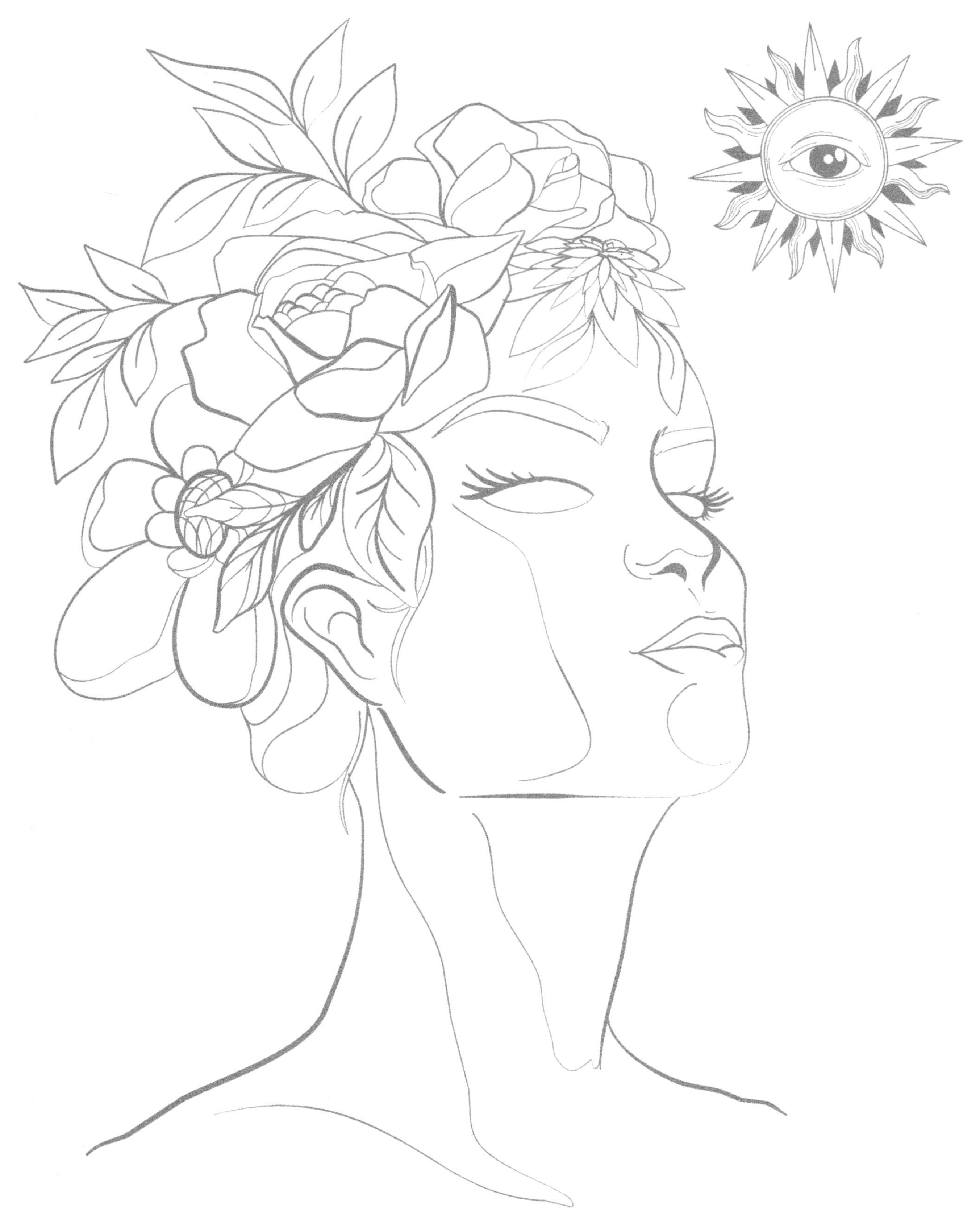

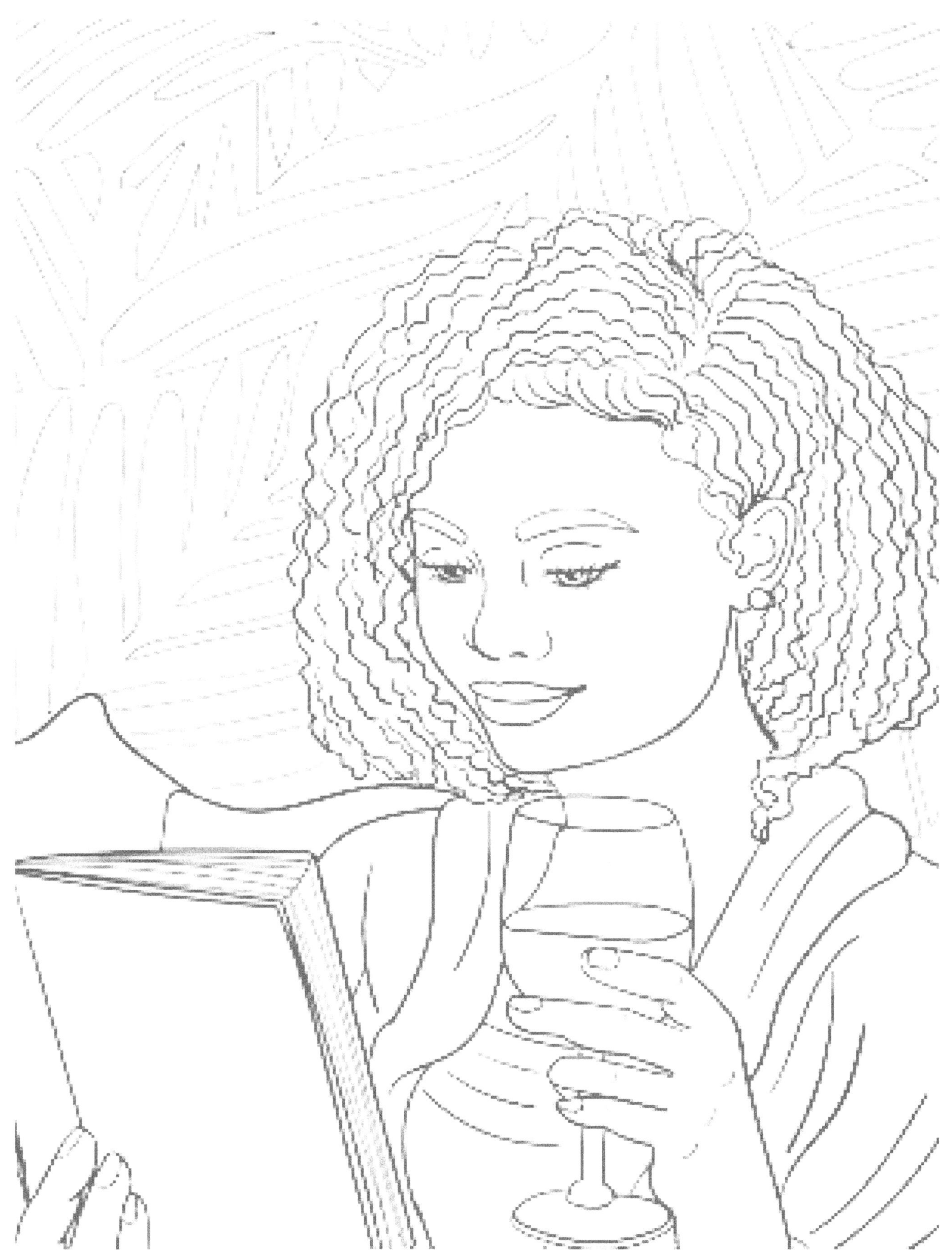

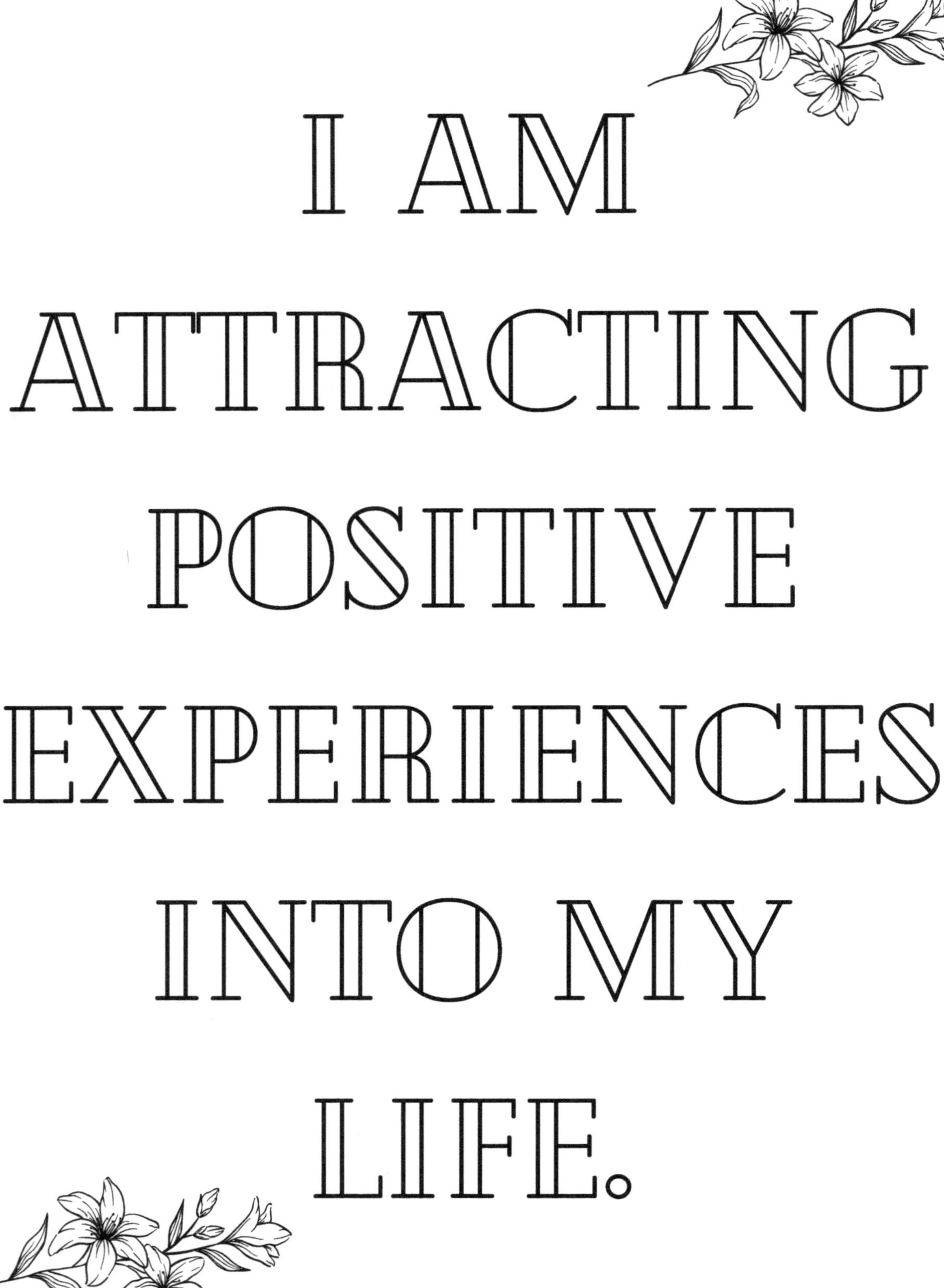

I AM
ATTRACTING
POSITIVE
EXPERIENCES
INTO MY
LIFE.

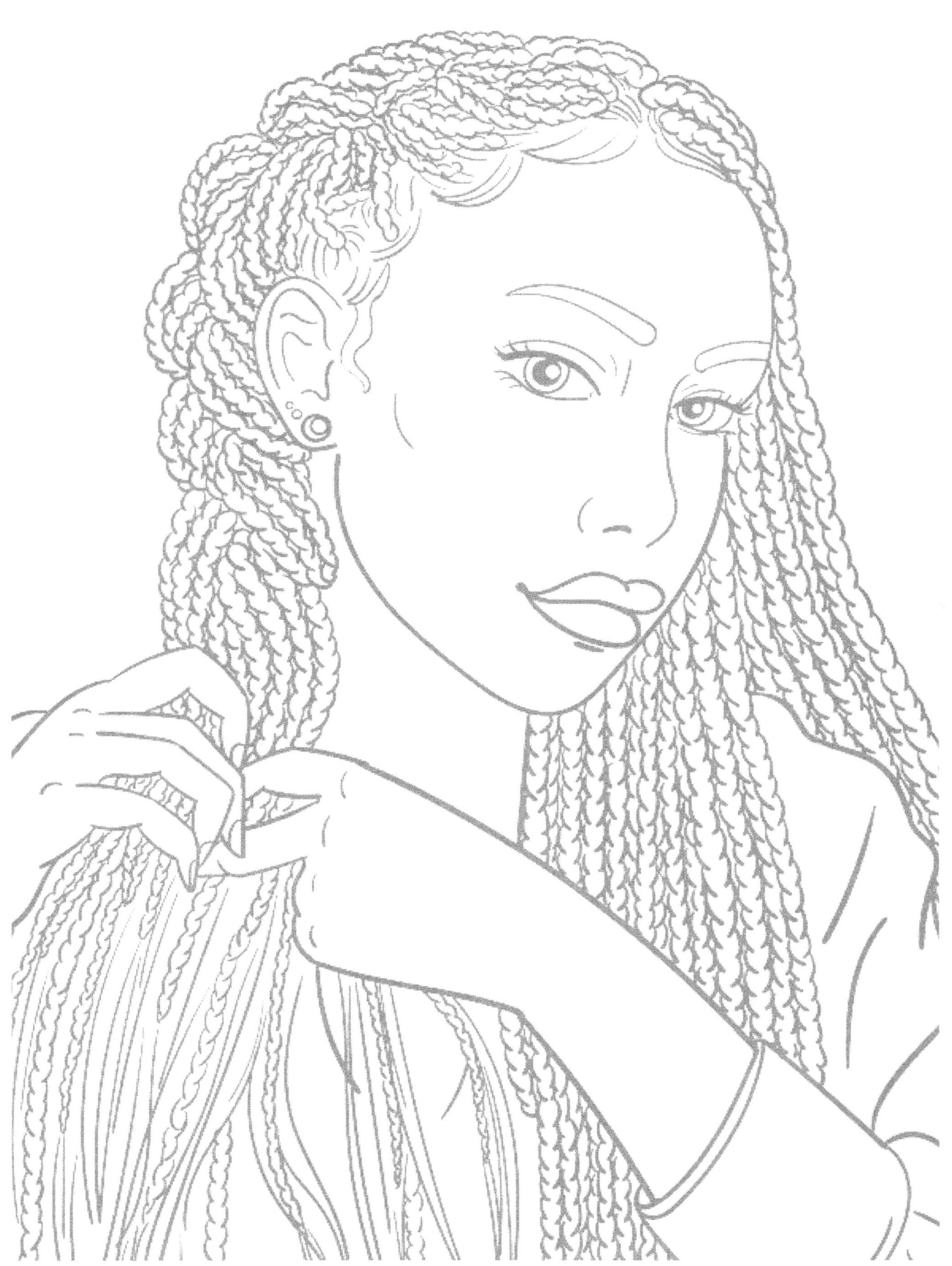

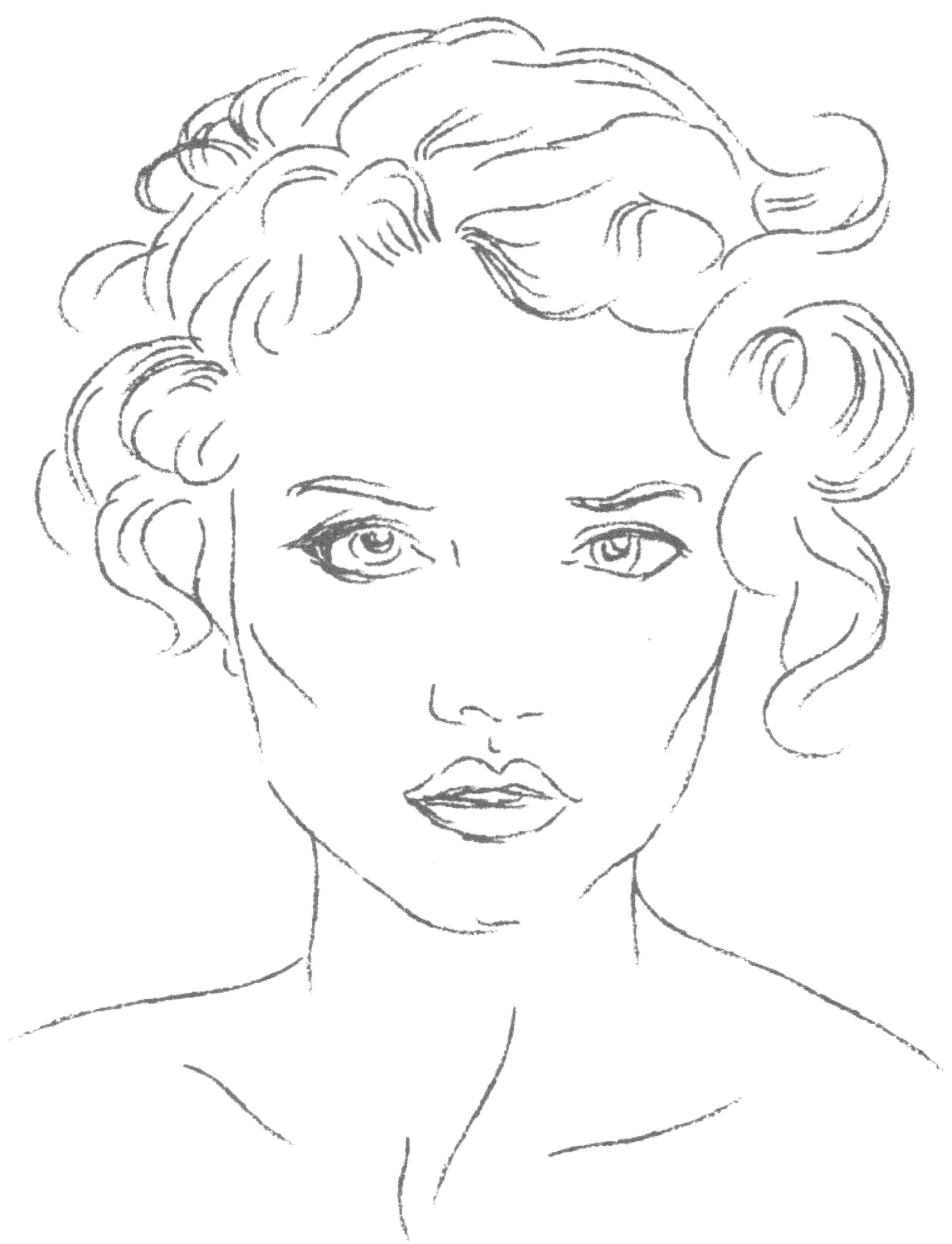

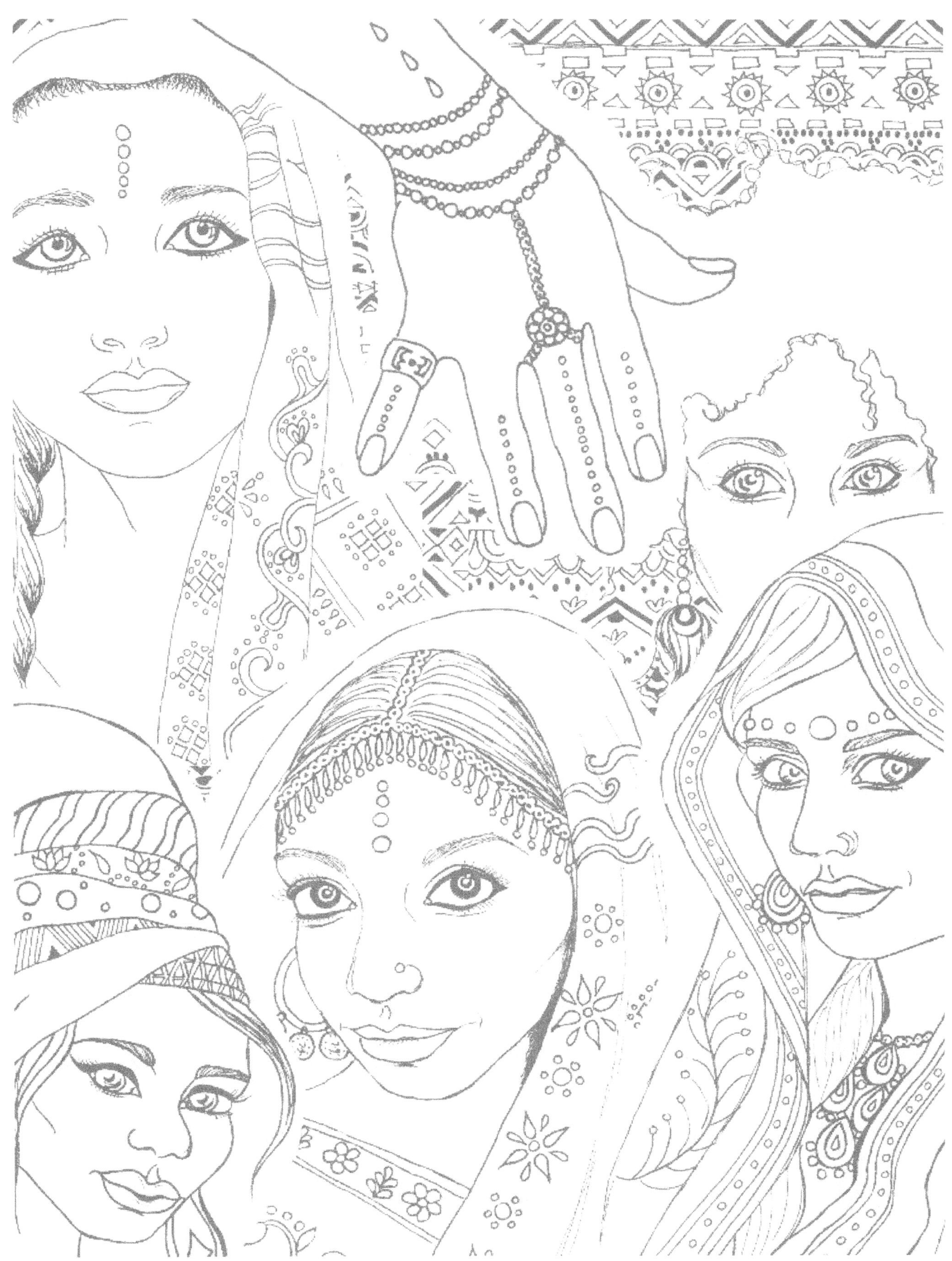

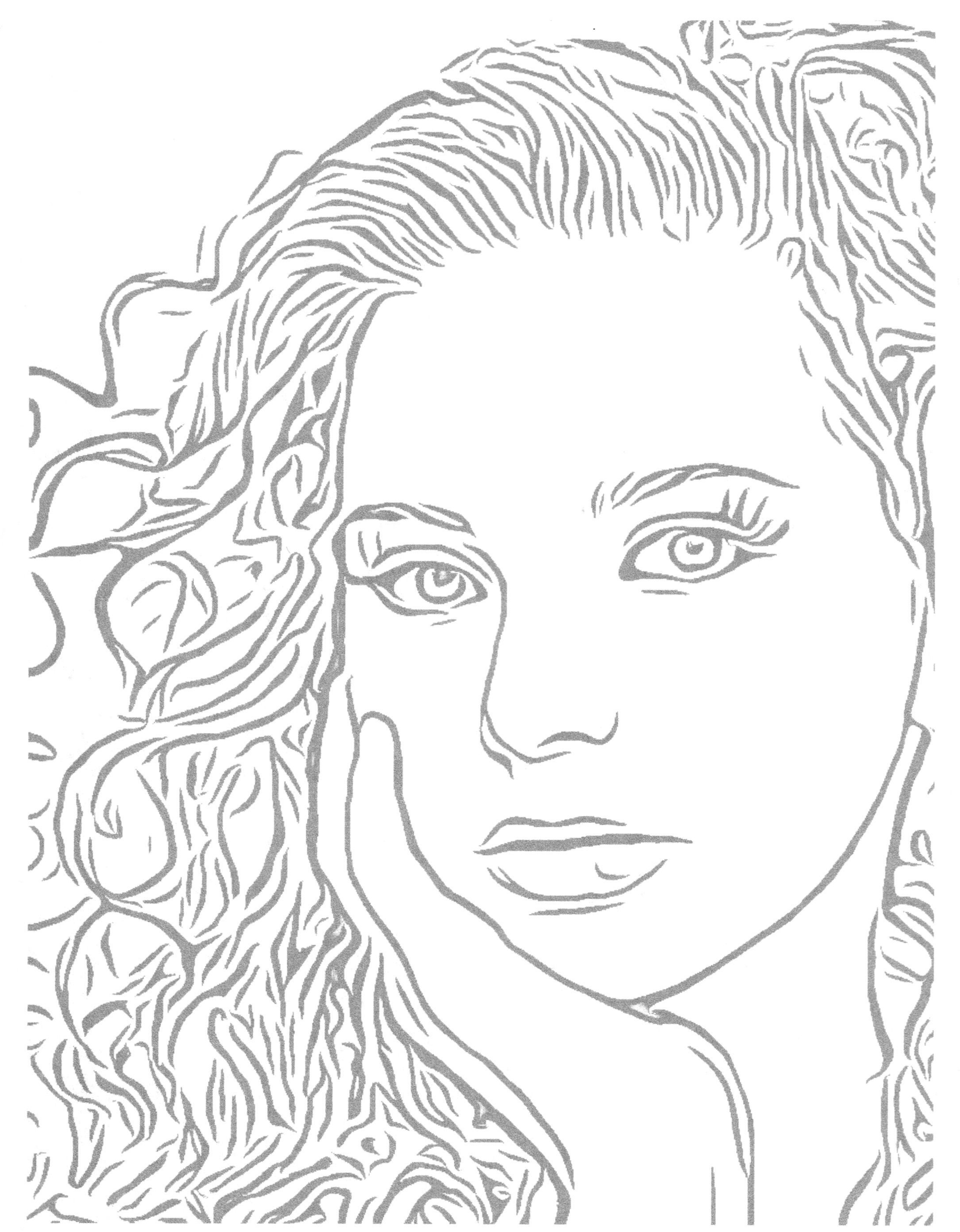

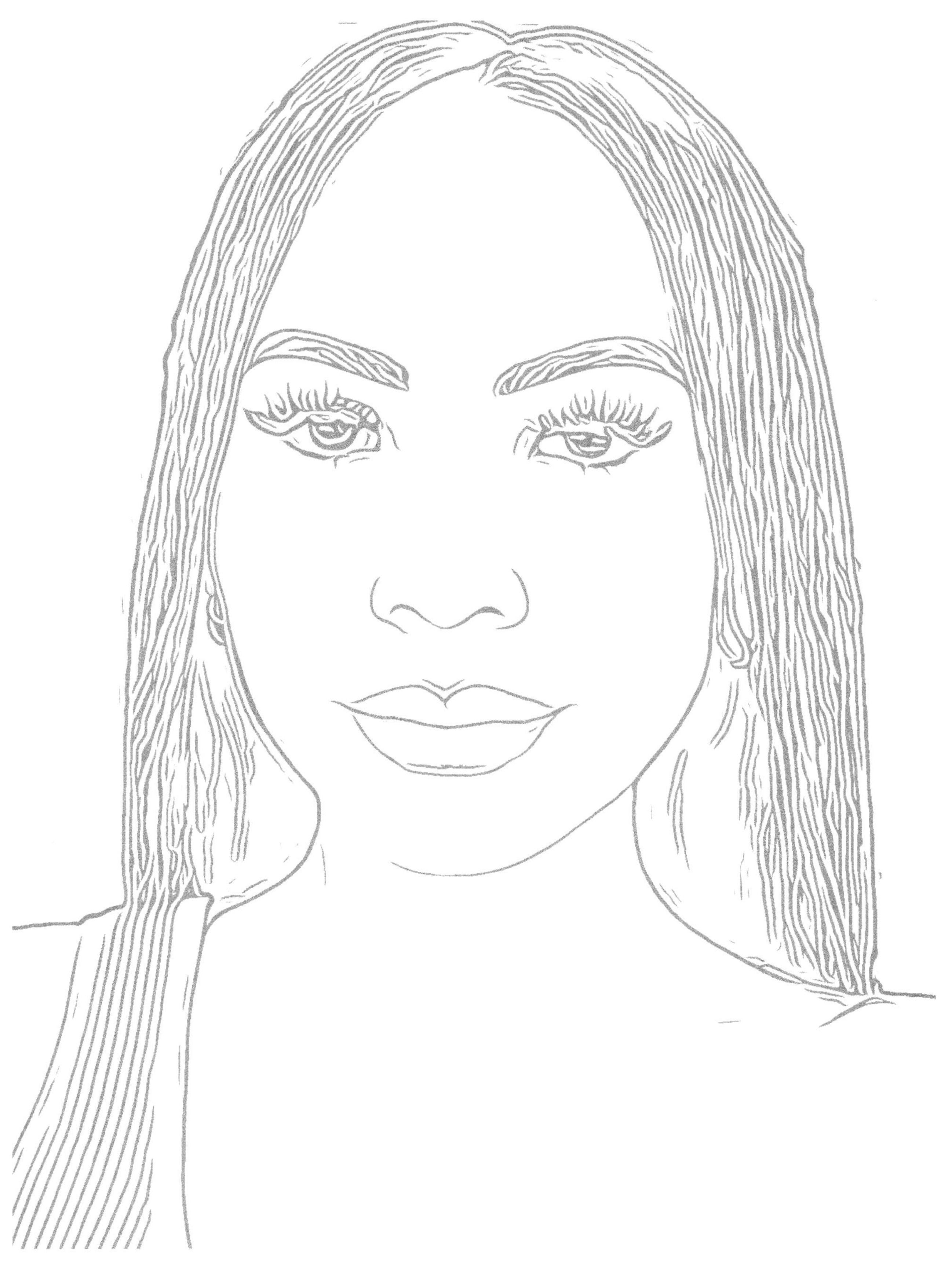

THINK
BELIEVE
DREAM
AND DARE

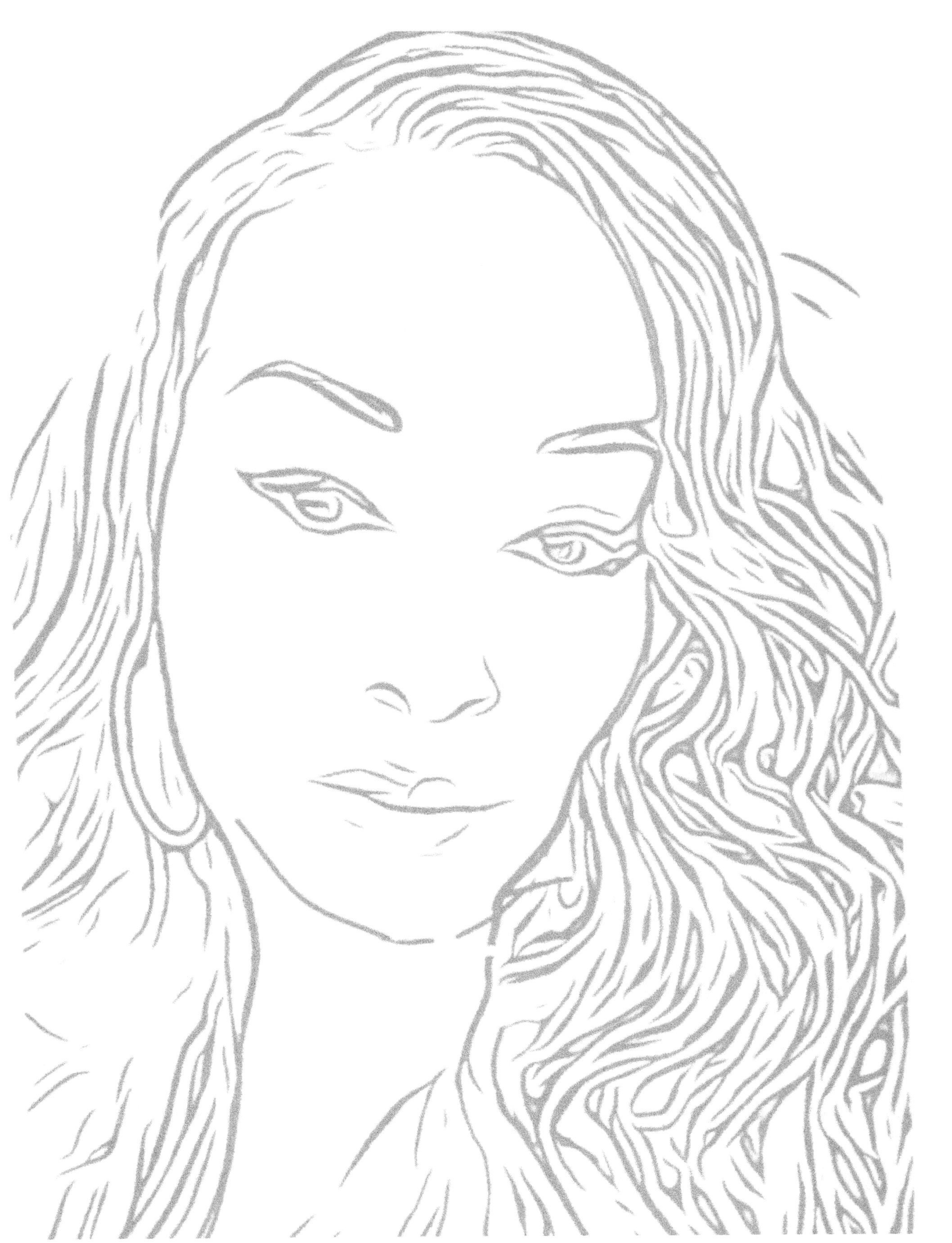

www.ingramcontent.com/pod-product-compliance
Lightning Source LLC
Chambersburg PA
CBHW060610120726
48002CB00010B/2904